THE COMPLETE ADVOCATE II: EMPLOYMENT OFFENSES IN HEALTH CARE CONTEXTS

A Practice File for Representing Clients from Beginning to End

THE COMPLETE ADVOCATE II: EMPLOYMENT OFFENSES IN HEALTH CARE CONTEXTS

A Practice File for Representing Clients from Beginning to End

A.G. Harmon, J.D., Ph.D.
Clinical Associate Professor
The Columbus School of Law
The Catholic University of America
Washington, D.C.

CAROLINA ACADEMIC PRESS

Durham, North Carolina

ISBN: 978-0-7698-5578-3 (print)
ISBN: 978-0-3271-7978-8 (ebook)

Library of Congress Cataloging-in-Publication Data

Harmon, A. G., 1962- author.
   The complete advocate II : employment offenses in health care contexts : a practice file for representing clients from beginning to end / A.G. Harmon, J.D., Ph.D., The Columbus School of Law, The Catholic University of America, Washington, D.C.
   p. cm.
   ISBN 978-0-7698-5578-3
   1. Practice of law—United States. 2. Attorney and client—United States. 3. Trial practice—United States. I. Title.
      KF300.H368 2013
      344.7301'76161—dc23

2013024269

Carolina Academic Press, LLC
700 Kent Street
Durham, North Carolina 27701
Telephone (919) 489-7486
Fax (919) 493-5668
www.caplaw.com

Printed in the United States of America
2018 Printing

TABLE OF CONTENTS

ACKNOWLEDGMENTS

The author would like to thank the faculty and staff of The Columbus School of Law at The Catholic University of America for their support, particularly Lisa Everhart, Beverly Jennison, Frederick Woods, Victor Williams, and Olivia Farrar. He would also like to acknowledge the research assistance of Nate Sloan, Jessica DeSimone, Derek Karchner, Sam Widdoes, Brett Sandford, and Victoria Kawecki, and the editorial assistance of Jennifer A. Beszley of LexisNexis.

INTRODUCTION

A common complaint about law school is that students are not given the big picture. They learn bits and pieces of the law—some theory, some practice, some skills—but are never quite sure how, where, or especially when, a particular piece of knowledge fits into the overall task of a client's representation. In other words, despite their education, they seldom get a bird's eye view of the entire process, from start to finish, so that they can see all the dimensions that a legal problem might entail.

Like its predecessor text (*The Complete Advocate*, LexisNexis 2010, which concerned age discrimination and professional responsibility matters) *The Complete Advocate II: Employment Offenses in Health Care Contexts*, is designed to guide a student through all aspects of a legal process: researching an area of law, filing pleadings, writing and arguing motions, proposing settlement, and pursuing and arguing appeals—from the beginning of the process to the end. The case file includes intake memos and assignments, for the purpose of drafting pleadings; a variety of litigation documents—depositions, affidavits, and exhibits—for the purpose of preparing litigation memoranda; motions and orders of the district court, for the purpose of filing an appeal; and even private, confidential facts (in the Teacher's Manual) for use in mediation sessions and trial practice. The text's purpose is not only to provide students with an education in the substantive and procedural dimensions of the subject matter, but also to provide them with a paradigm for practice—a conceptual model from which they can pattern their future approaches to a litigation matter, regardless of its type. Having "seen" and experienced the development of a case from its first step to its final resolution, students will have a fair estimation of what needs to be done throughout the course of a matter, and can gain a surer footing and orientation as to where they are when brought into the middle of an ongoing lawsuit. This complete view of the legal landscape—from inception to conclusion—is portable knowledge that can be transferred to the nature of any particular enterprise.

The facts of the cases, set in the Tenth Circuit, revolve around the federal False Claims Act (FCA) and the federal Anti-Kickback Statute (AKS). The FCA suit involves a twenty-nine-year-old medical records specialist, Grace Garrett, suing her former employer, Twin Oaks Hospital, a three hundred-bed health facility in Overland Park, Kansas. Garrett claims that the hospital, through its employees Charles McRaney, Coding Supervisor, and Rosemary Rinehart, Hospital Administrator, knowingly coded a series of "basic pneumonia" cases from a nearby retirement facility as the more serious "severe pneumococcal pneumonia." The result was an unjust enrichment for the hospital, a fact that Garrett says she uncovered and brought to the attention of the Health and Human Services Department. This would entitle her to a portion of the claim as a "whistleblower." The hospital has several defenses to this claim, ranging from standing arguments to merits arguments.

In addition, Garrett has asked her attorneys to look into possible claims against McRaney and the hospital for intentional infliction of emotional distress and defamation. Further, McRaney wants to know whether he has any defense against a false imprisonment claim under Kansas law, and also how a potential malicious prosecution claim would stand up against Garrett.

Twin Oaks Hospital's woes continue in a separate claim involving an alleged kickback scheme between it and a local medical practice, The Crenshaw Group. Dr. David E. Barrier, an orthopedic surgeon on staff at Twin Oaks, alleges that the hospital knowingly sponsored a series of health fairs at retirement facilities owned by The Crenshaw Group. He further alleges the group referred its geriatric patients back to the hospital. If established, the claim would entitle Dr. Barrier to a share of the recovery as the whistleblower. The hospital responds with a series of defenses.

Pleadings, discovery, motions and briefs, client correspondence, and settlement negotiations, are all dimensions of the text. The assignments are ordered so that students may gain the full perspective of the advocate. In addition, all assignments are written from the perspective of one of the law firms representing the parties.

The chief advantage of the multi-dimensional approach of this book is that it can be used to teach a variety of skills involving the same fact situation. A professor may custom design the focus of the class in terms of the substantive area, the scope of the research, and the types of assignments chosen. Versatility is a hallmark.

Dates

To prevent the text from becoming out of date, dates are set out according to the following key:

The current year = YEAR (e.g., January 1, YEAR)

A year before the current year = YR-1 (e.g. January 1, YR-1)

Two years before the current year = YR-2 (e.g. January 1, YR-2), etc.

A year *from* the current year = YR+1 (January 1, YR+1)

Two years *from* the current year = YR+2 (e.g. January 1, YR+2); etc.

Pagination

The book is paginated consecutively; however, documents for use in the two Motion's Brief assignments—Assignments #7 and #14—are also paginated in the top right corner, so that they can be assembled as a record on appeal. The Complaint and Answer for each of the two appellate problems are included in the Teacher's Manual, in the event the professor would like to assign pleadings drafting exercises—Assignments #6 and #13. When the appellate record is assembled, it should accord with the pagination at the beginning of the Complaint, top right corner, and proceed in order as the documents dictate. References to the record in each of the two Bench Briefs relate to this pagination scheme.

GARRETT v. TWIN OAKS HOSPITAL, INC.: PARTIES/PRINCIPALS

Stuart Chamberlin, candidate for U.S. Congress

Grace Garrett, 29, Medical Records Specialist, Twin Oaks Hospital

Christopher Heller, Investigations Officer, HHS

Claire Heller, wife of Christopher Heller, KC Payroll Services

Robert Jackson, 40, Assistant Coding Supervisor, Twin Oaks Hospital

Charles McRaney, 55, Coding Supervisor, Twin Oaks Hospital

Walter Ridley, 85, resident of River Crest Retirement Community

Rosemary Rinehart, 59, Hospital Administrator, Twin Oaks Hospital

Leslie Ross, Mid-West Health Insurance, Medicare Intermediary

Amanda Stevenson, secretary, Twin Oaks Hospital

Sarah Wright, secretary to McRaney and Jackson, Twin Oaks Hospital

BARRIER v. TWIN OAKS HOSPITAL, INC.: PARTIES/PRINCIPALS

David Barrier, M.D., 41, orthopedic surgeon, Overland Park Bone and Joint Clinic

Andrew Crenshaw, M.D., 61, managing partner of The Crenshaw Group

Julia Courtland, 40, former Director of Hospital Services, Twin Oaks Hospital

Barry Farr, Chief Financial Officer, Twin Oaks Hospital

Clark Milner, M.D.: Partner, The Crenshaw Group; Brother of Rosemary Rinehart

Rosemary Rinehart, 59, Hospital Administrator, Twin Oaks Hospital

Dan Webster, Compliance Officer, Twin Oaks Hospital

Assignment 1

CLOSED UNIVERSE MEMORANDUM

From: Senior Attorney
To: Junior Associate
Date: Today, YEAR
Re: Grace Garrett matter

Grace Garrett, a twenty-nine-year-old Medical Records Specialist with Twin Oaks Hospital in Overland Park, Kansas, came to our office about an incident that occurred two weeks ago.

On a Wednesday afternoon, around 5:00 p.m., Garrett was at her desk reviewing some files. Her job, which she's had for one year, consists of inputting data with regard to hospital charges. Garrett's regular work hours are from 9:00 a.m. to 5:00 p.m., but she was allowed to work a certain amount of overtime every month upon obtaining the approval of her supervisor, Charles McRaney. He had always given his approval in the past, whether it was obtained beforehand or after-the-fact, as long as the hours were within the cap. That afternoon, Garrett had not obtained prior approval, but decided to stay an extra hour to catch up on some things. Her children—ages five and seven—were at a school function that would end at 6:30 p.m., so she had to leave at 6:00 p.m. to pick them up.

As she was making her way through the work, she noticed that some of the files contained discrepancies between the charges and the actual procedures done, something she'd noticed several times over the past few months. She'd spoken to McRaney about it, but he'd always shrug off the matter and say he would look into it on a program in the medical records office—one to which Garrett did not have access. He had not gotten back to her yet when she noticed a similar problem in the new files that afternoon.

No one picked up the phone when Garrett called his office, and then she remembered that McRaney was on a three-day vacation. At that point, because she couldn't complete her work without an answer, she decided to see if his secretary, Sarah Wright, could help her. Wright was just about to leave for the day. She agreed to leave her computer on so that Garrett could check the records. After Wright left, no one besides Garrett was in the coding office.

Wright's office is a twelve-by-twelve room with a large, casement-style window on one wall. There is one door into the room from the main part of the office—which is the way that Garrett entered—and another door on the opposite wall, which leads to a large filing room. This door was closed. The desk sits against the windowless wall (see attached diagram provided by Garrett). Garrett sat down at the desk, booted up the coding program, and began to download some files to her flash drive, so that she could take them back to her own work area.

After a few minutes, the door to her right—the one to the filing room—opened. McRaney came in with a file in his hand. He was startled when he saw Garrett there and asked her what she was doing. Garrett herself was also startled, since McRaney was not expected back until the next day. When she explained that she was just checking on the records problem they'd discussed, McRaney became agitated. He turned and called behind him, shouting for his Assistant Supervisor, Robert Jackson, and made a motion with his arm—as though telling him to go around to the other side of Wright's office. He then told Garrett that she was violating Hospital protocol by trespassing in an area where she had no permission to be.

4

Garrett, surprised, answered that Wright had given her permission to use her computer, and that she was working overtime. McRaney, shouting, said that Wright answered to him, that Garrett was probably lying, and that he had not approved any overtime. He wondered if she was the one pirating expensive software from the office, an occurrence about which there was a staff meeting about a week before. Garrett had attended the meeting, at which McRaney shouted the entire time.

At that point, Jackson came to stand in the door from the main office. He leaned against one side of the frame and placed his hand against the other. McRaney then told Garrett to delete whatever she had saved to her flash drive or she would risk losing her job. Angry at his tone, she refused, denying any wrongdoing. Again, McRaney demanded that she delete the files, adding that the men would not leave the room—and neither would Garrett—until she complied. Garrett refused once more. McRaney then took his cell phone from his pocket and said he was calling security. He said it was his intention to keep her there until the security matter was addressed.

Garrett stood up to leave, saying that this was ridiculous and she would be late to pick up her children. McRaney then moved towards her, shoving a pointed finger at her and demanding she sit down. He also motioned to Jackson, who slammed the door behind him. When McRaney got through to security, he told the guards to come immediately, as there was a trespasser in the records room, trying to steal documents. When McRaney hung up, Garrett repeated that she had to leave to get her young children. They would be alone outside the school. McRaney said she was not going anywhere until she first deleted the files, and even then not until security came. He also threatened to call the police.

Garrett became visibly distraught and pled with McRaney. Recently, she's gone through a fierce custody battle with her ex-husband. He has of late threatened to steal the children and take them out of state. McRaney knew all of this and of Garrett's heightened concern for her children's safety, though he did not know that Garrett has been seeing a physician about insomnia and anxiety attacks. Still, the more Garrett pled and reminded him of the situation, the angrier he got. Every time Garrett tried to take a step, the men blocked her way. They would not let her use the phone to call the school about her children.

When security arrived, McRaney told the officer that Garrett had broken into the office and was stealing files. She tried to explain her side, but was so upset about the time—it was already 6:30 p.m., and the school is a twenty minute drive from work—she broke down and surrendered the drive to McRaney. He told the security officers to question her, and apparently also called the police, as they arrived soon thereafter. It was another twenty minutes before Garrett was allowed to leave. She was unable to reach anyone at the school as she drove. On the way, she had to pull over, incapacitated by a panic attack. She had never had an attack in the car before. A state trooper spotted her there and called an ambulance. Since this incident, she has had several more panic attacks associated with driving, which she says increases her fear about being able to reach her children.

Garrett says McRaney is known among the staff to have a wild temper. Many times over the last eight months he's publicly cursed at her for taking off to attend divorce and custody hearings, and threatened poor evaluations for what he characterized as her incessant "maternity leave."

McRaney is 55 years old; he is 6 ft. tall and weighs 180 lbs. Jackson is 40 years old, 5 ft. 10 in. tall and weighs 170 lbs. Garrett is 5 ft. 6 in. tall and weighs 115 lbs.

Under Kansas law, does Garrett have a case against McRaney for the tort of Intentional Infliction of Emotional Distress? For the purposes of your analysis, use the following case: *Taiwo v. Vu*, 822 P.2d 1024 (1991). For your analysis of whether the conduct is "intentional," use the following definition from the <u>Restatement (Second) of Torts</u> (1965):*

<u>Restatement (Second) of Torts</u> § 46

> *Intention and recklessness.* The rule stated in this Section applies where the actor desires to inflict severe emotional distress, and also where he knows that such distress is certain, or substantially certain, to result from his conduct. It applies also where he acts recklessly, as that term is defined in§ 500 [below], in deliberate disregard of a high degree of probability that the emotional distress will follow.

<u>Restatement (Second) of Torts</u> § 500

> The actor's conduct is in reckless disregard of the safety of another if he does an act or intentionally fails to do an act which it is his duty to the other to do, knowing or having reason to know of facts which would lead a reasonable man to realize, not only that his conduct creates an unreasonable risk of physical harm to another, but also that such risk is substantially greater than that which is necessary to make his conduct negligent.

Illustrations from Restatement § 46:

15. During A's absence from her home, B attempts to commit suicide in A's kitchen by cutting his throat. B knows that A is substantially certain to return and find his body, and to suffer emotional distress. A finds B lying in her kitchen in a pool of gore, and suffers severe emotional distress. B is subject to liability to A.

16. The same facts as in Illustration 15, except that B does not know that A is substantially certain to find him, but does know that there is a high degree of probability that she will do so. B is subject to liability to A.

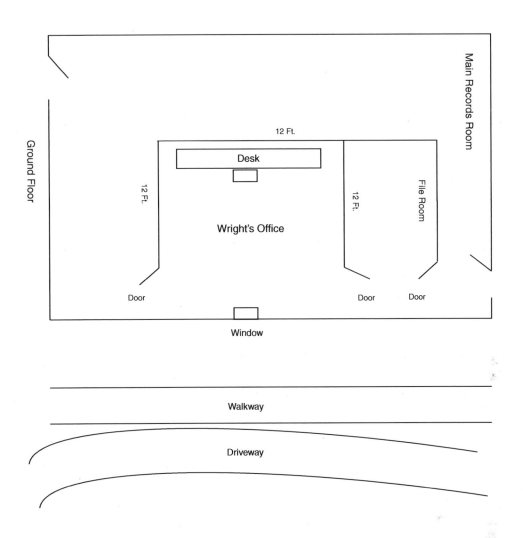

CLOSED UNIVERSE MEMORANDUM

From: Senior Attorney
To: Junior Associate
Date: Today, YEAR
Re: Charles McRaney matter

Charles McRaney, the fifty-five-year-old Coding Supervisor at Twin Oaks Hospital in Overland Park, Kansas, called us yesterday about an incident that occurred two weeks ago. As head of the office, McRaney is in charge of a staff that associates each medical procedure performed at the Hospital with a specific code derived from a universal classification system; these codes are used for billing purposes. The facts of the incident involve McRaney and two other Hospital employees: Robert Jackson, the forty-year-old Assistant Coding Supervisor; and Grace Garrett, a twenty-nine-year-old Medical Records Specialist.

At 6:00 p.m., McRaney was returning from a three-day vacation when he decided to stop by his office in the Hospital to pick up a jacket he'd left there. He got off the elevator and started down the hall when he saw that Jackson was still in his office next door. McRaney and Jackson's secretary, Sarah Wright, whose office is in the records room a few doors away, had left with the other coding staff at the regular time, 5:00 p.m.

After McRaney and Jackson talked for a few minutes, McRaney picked up his jacket, then decided to stop by the records room to return some files that had been left on his desk. He asked Jackson to wait for him in the hall so that they could walk out to their cars together.

Wright's office is a twelve-by-twelve room with a large, casement-style window on one wall. There is one door into the room from the main part of the records room, and another door on the opposite wall, which leads to the file room. This door was closed. The desk sits against the windowless wall. (See attached sketch provided by McRaney.)

McRaney entered the records room from the hall, and then entered the file room. Once there, he heard a noise coming from Wright's office. He opened the door and found Garrett at Wright's desk, using Wright's computer. Garrett looked surprised. McRaney knew that she was supposed to have left the Hospital at 5:00 p.m. He had not given her permission to work overtime, as he was out of town, but in the past he had always granted her overtime whether she asked for it beforehand or after the fact.

McRaney asked what Garrett was doing at Wright's desk. Garrett minimized the program and said that she was just looking for some records on Wright's computer that she had asked him for over the last few weeks. Since he was gone and she needed them for a deadline, she had decided to work overtime and to get permission to use the computer from Wright.

McRaney then noticed that Garrett was in the process of downloading something from Wright's computer onto a USB flash drive. He immediately became suspicious. There had been thefts of expensive software from the records department over the past few months, potentially compromising private patient data. The Hospital risked liability, and Hospital Administrator Rosemary Rinehart had just that week charged McRaney with investigating the matter and putting a stop to the thefts. She had authorized McRaney and Jackson to police the matter personally with the utmost vigilance, but with discretion, keeping the matter in-house. Rinehart added that McRaney would be held responsible if the thieves were successful again.

McRaney also had a personal stake in the matter. A part-time software developer, he had designed proprietary records management software for the Hospital, which owns the rights and licenses it to other healthcare institutions, physicians' offices, nursing homes, etc., for use in managing their insurance claims. The Hospital offers the software licenses for purchase exclusively online through its website, and the licensing transactions take place through Wright's computer. Other than Wright's, the only other computer with the software installed on it belongs to McRaney himself.

McRaney stood in the file room door and called out for Jackson. When Jackson entered the records room, McRaney motioned for him to go around to the other end of Wright's office. As McRaney continued to question Garrett, Jackson appeared in the other door and stood there.

McRaney told Garrett she wasn't supposed to be in Wright's office, and then asked if she was stealing the software. Garrett became defensive, denied the accusation, and said that Wright had given her permission to use the computer. McRaney then demanded that Garrett give him the flash drive she was using. Garrett refused. He demanded that she delete the files that she was downloading, but she refused again. McRaney said that Garrett could not leave the office until she surrendered the drive. He then took out his cell phone and said he would call security. Garrett replied that she wasn't afraid and would be glad to prove how wrong he was.

After a few more minutes of back-and-forth between Garrett and McRaney, she got up and started towards him. She said, "This is ridiculous. I have to go get my sons at school." McRaney then walked towards her, blocking the way. He pointed her back to the chair. Garrett retreated and sat down once more. Jackson slammed the door behind him, and McRaney did the same with the door behind him.

When McRaney reached security, he told the guards to come immediately, as there was a trespasser in the records room trying to steal documents. Garrett then became visibly upset. She repeated that she had to leave to get her young children, ages five and seven. They would be alone outside the school. McRaney said she could leave as soon as she gave him the drive and talked to security. He said that if she didn't, he would call the police as well.

Recently, Garrett has gone through a fierce custody battle with her ex-husband, and he has of late made threats to steal the children and take them out of state. She says McRaney knew all of this and of her heightened concern for the children's safety. She also says he knew she was seeing a physician about insomnia and anxiety attacks. He says he only knew about general threats Garrett's husband had made, but nothing else.

When Garrett asked to use the phone to call the school about her children, McRaney said no. In the past, she was always threatening to call the press when her husband was giving her trouble. He feared she might do that in this situation too, and his boss wouldn't appreciate the publicity, especially considering the compromised records problem that might be exposed.

Security arrived ten minutes later. McRaney told the officer that Garrett was stealing files. Garrett then broke down and surrendered the drive to McRaney. He told the security officers to question her and write up a report that he expected to see the next day. As he was leaving, he announced that he

11

was going to call the police after all. He did so because he was unsure of his legal obligations if a crime was involved—stealing thousands of dollars worth of software as well as patient records. It was around 6:30 p.m. at that time. After both the security guard and police interrogations, Garrett could not leave until 7:00 p.m. It is a twenty-minute drive from the Hospital to the school that Garrett's sons attend.

McRaney has since learned that Garrett's children were at an after-school program, and that she was unable to reach anyone at the school as she drove. On the way, she had to pull over on the busy interstate, incapacitated by a panic attack. She has never had a panic attack in the car before. A state trooper finally arrived and called an ambulance. Since this incident, Garrett has had several more panic attacks associated with driving, which she says increases her fear about being able to reach her children.

Upon investigation, the USB drive did not contain the software. McRaney admits he has a reputation for a bad temper. He was resentful of Garrett's recent absences from work due to her custody hearings, and that night he had hoped the incident would result in her official reprimand by the Hospital Administrator. Occasionally, he had required Garrett to make up the time she missed by staying late at work.

Assuming that Garrett brings a claim of false imprisonment against McRaney, does he have a statutory defense?

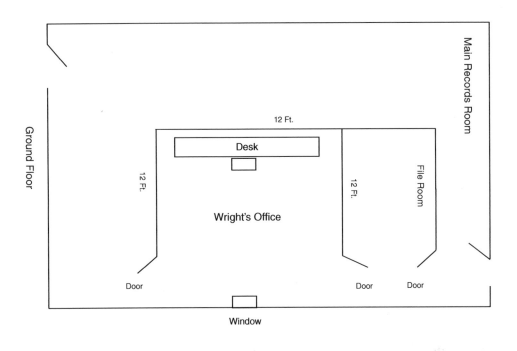

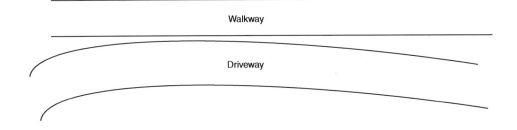

OPEN UNIVERSE MEMORANDUM

To: New Associate
From: Senior Attorney
Re: Grace Garrett—Defamation Claim
Date: Today, YEAR

Today, I met with again with Grace Garrett. Something new has come up with regard to her employment situation. Although Ms. Garrett is still working at Twin Oaks Hospital, the employment relationship there has been strained since the incident with her supervisor, Charles McRaney.

Ms. Garrett relayed that the company had its annual picnic at a local park two weeks ago. There, a conversation was held among members of the hospital management, portions of which she believes defamed her. The conversation was captured on a cell phone video file. Though not recorded with prior permission, there is no evidentiary objection in Kansas on those grounds.

I've attached the transcript of the client interview. At this point, I want you to focus on whether either of the two statements made by Mr. McRaney is covered by the defense of qualified privilege under Kansas law. In other words, assume that the prima facie case of defamation is met as to both statements; focus instead on whether each of those statements is covered by the qualified privilege defense under Kansas law.

In your overview paragraph, explain what kind of standard (actual malice, negligence, etc.) would apply if the statements are privileged and what standard would apply if they are not, but do not yet examine whether the statements actually meet the pertinent standards.

For now, assume that the statements made by Charles McRaney, related in the transcript, are two separate statements (not one continuous statement), each with defamatory potential. The first statement begins on Line 247 and ends on Line 251. The second statement begins on Line 287 and ends on Line 292.

Finally, assume that Ms. Garrett is not a public figure.

Provide me with a memo on this matter.

1   Client Interview: Grace Garrett, Potential Defamation claim (File No. WS-4923)
2
3   Mr. Sheffield: This is a client interview with Grace Garret, at the Overland Park, Kansas office of
4   Sheffield and Major. The date is October 13, YEAR. It's 10:00 A.M. Present are myself, William
5   Sheffield—Ms. Garrett, our client—and our stenographer, Clayton Marshall.
6
7   Q: Ms. Garrett, would you state your full name, age, and address?
8
9   A: Grace Anne Garrett, 29. I live at 2394 McAllister Boulevard, Overland Park, Kansas.
10
11   Q: And you're still employed by Twin Oaks Hospital here in town?
12
13   A: Right now, I am.
14
15   Q: What do you mean, "right now"?
16
17   A: Because I'm not sure how long I'll be staying there, after all that's happened over the past
18   few months.
19
20   Q: But you haven't stopped working there yet?
21
22   A: No.
23
24   Q: And you haven't given notice either?
25
26   A: No.
27
28   Q: All right then. Before we turn to all that's transpired at work lately, I need a bit more basic
29   information from you. You've been a Medical Records Specialist at Twin Oaks for about a
30   year, isn't that right?
31
32   A: Yes.
33
34   Q: Tell me more about that position. What exactly is a "medical records specialist"?
35
36   A: Well, among other things, I place a pre-assigned code on each procedure performed at the
37   hospital, and on all therapies, prescriptions—that kind of thing—so that it can be submitted
38   to the various entities to be charged for the work done.
39
40   Q: Have you held a similar position in that regard anywhere else?
41
42   A: Other than at Twin Oaks?
43
44   Q: Yes.
45
46   A: I worked in the same capacity for a year at another hospital here in town—St. Michael's—
47   before that.
48
49   Q: How many records coordinators are there at Twin Oaks?
50
51   A: Ten, including me.
52
53   Q: And you report to Mr. McRaney as your supervisor, correct?
54
55   A: Yes.
56
57   Q: His position again?
58
59   A: He's the Coding Supervisor. He's in charge of us all, in addition to some other
60   responsibilities.

61	Q:	All right. Now, of course we're aware of your incident with Mr. McRaney last August. But
62		just for the context, I'll read a summary of it so that it can be a part of this transcript, okay?
63		Just in case it has some bearing on the new matter that you've brought to us today?
64		
65	A:	That's fine.
66		
67	Q:	Good. You claim that on the evening of August 12, YEAR, while on unapproved overtime,
68		Mr. McRaney came upon you at another employee's computer after work.
69		
70	A:	That's right, except that whenever I submitted a request in the past, whether beforehand or
71		after the fact, my overtime was always approved by Mr. McRaney.
72		
73	Q:	I understand. Still, it wasn't approved beforehand that night. Correct?
74		
75	A:	No.
76		
77	Q:	And you were at that computer because you'd received permission from a secretary in
78		Mr. McRaney's office to check some records. Mr. McRaney came into that office, accused you
79		of pirating software—an occurrence that had happened late at the hospital —and called
80		his assistant supervisor, Robert Jackson. The two men blocked the only exits to the room.
81		Although you explained your circumstances, Mr. McRaney demanded that you delete the
82		files you were working on. When you refused, he called security. You were late picking up
83		your children, and because of your fear for their safety—due to your ex-husband's recent
84		threats to kidnap the children—your heightened anxiety about them was exacerbated
85		by the situation. Mr.McRaney knew all this, you claim, but refused to let you leave or to
86		call the school until security came. He also threatened to call the police. Anxious to leave,
87		you surrendered the drive upon which you were copying the files. Nevertheless, you were
88		detained because of the security interrogation, as well as by questioning from the police,
89		and had a debilitating panic attack on the way to the school. Although you'd been seeing
90		a physician about anxiety attacks and insomnia before this incident, you claim that you'd
91		never had any attacks associated with driving until then. You've had similar recurrences
92		since that time. Is that a fair summary?
93		
94	A:	Yes. By and large, it is.
95		
96	Q:	Now, all that occurred on August 12th. What's happened since that time?
97		
98	A:	Well, the security report was sent to the Hospital Administrator, Rosemary Rinehart.
99		She called me in and we talked about it. She'd been given the drive by Charles, and the
100		two of them realized that what he'd accused me of was untrue. I was most certainly
101		not pirating software. On top of that, Sarah Wright—the secretary who let me use her
102		computer—confirmed my story. So Ms. Rinehart had Charles join us. While he was there,
103		she apologized about the whole affair getting out of hand. She went on to say that things
104		had been on edge lately because of the software theft—and the potential liability it can
105		expose the hospital to. Because of that, she'd asked Charles and the other supervisors
106		to be particularly vigilant about matters of protocol. Unfortunately, that was why things
107		escalated to the degree that they had that night.
108		
109	Q:	And what did Mr. McRaney say?
110		
111	A:	He agreed with her, but he wouldn't look at me while he spoke. He just stared at the wall
112		or at the carpet the whole time. If you ask me, he was belligerent. I don't think he really
113		wanted to apologize at all.
114		
115	Q:	What happened then?
116		
117	A:	Then? What else could I do? I went back to work. I avoided Charles as best as I could
118		and tried to get things back to normal. Still, as you know, I was terrified that night.
119		They put me and my children in danger, and I'm still suffering from the effects. My panic

120		attacks—the ones associated with driving—have worsened since this latest business at the
121		company picnic.
122		
123	Q:	All right. Now, tell me about that event.
124		
125	A:	Well, two weeks ago we had a company picnic. It was the annual day-long affair at the
126		county park. Employees and their families. Food and games and prizes. I'm sure you're
127		familiar with such things?
128		
129	Q:	Yes.
130		
131	A:	I didn't go myself. I was too upset after all that had happened. I certainly didn't feel like
132		dealing with the awkwardness of running into Charles or Robert Jackson there.
133		
134	Q:	If you didn't go to the picnic, how do you have knowledge of what you're claiming was said
135		that day?
136		
137	A:	Because a friend of mine went. She was nearby and caught the whole incident—the
138		conversation I'm talking about—on her smart phone. I've had the file downloaded to my
139		computer and backed it up in several places. I have my computer with me, too, so I can show
140		you the file. The picture's a little fuzzy, but the sound is very clear. I can identify the voices
141		of everyone speaking.
142		
143	Q:	All right, but let's continue for a moment with the background of the event. You said your
144		friend recorded the conversation?
145		
146	A:	Yes. Amanda Stevenson. She works for Thomas LaGuard, the Assistant Administrator. She
147		went to the picnic with her two pre-school daughters.
148		
149	Q:	And what's the context for what I'm about to see? So I'll understand what I'm watching.
150		Who's present? Where are they speaking? Who's speaking to whom? That kind of thing.
151		
152	A:	Okay. What you're about to see is a table of people under one of the open tents they had at
153		the picnic. It was a big tent with lots of big tables. People sat there, from what Amanda told
154		me, when they were eating or when they just wanted to take a break. She said she and her
155		daughters came through the buffet line, then entered the tent area. There was a vacant
156		table in the back, so her group took it and began to have lunch. After about fifteen minutes,
157		several of the hospital management came up with their plates and took the table right next
158		to Amanda's.
159		
160	Q:	When you say "management," to whom are you referring?
161		
162	A:	Well, besides Charles McRaney, there was Rosemary Rinehart, the Hospital
163		Administrator, and Thomas LaGuard, Amanda's boss. Then there was Lisa Benedict,
164		the Hospital Services Coordinator, and Barry Farr, who's the Chief Financial Officer.
165		The group of them—save for one person who wasn't there—happen to make up the
166		Committee for Advancements at the hospital. There were some secretaries with them,
167		too—Rosemary's and Lisa's—and what looks like somebody's small children. It looks like
168		there are about nine or ten people in all, including the children. At least from what I've
169		been able to tell.
170		
171	Q:	What do you mean by the "Committee for Advancements"?
172		
173	A:	That's the committee that decides the internal affairs of the hospital, as far as raises
174		and promotions go. Ms. Rinehart is the head, of course, but the others have a vote as
175		well, Amanda tells me. The reason that matters to me is that I was up for a promotion to
176		Assistant Coding Supervisor—a job that Charles's assistant, Robert Jackson, had held. He's
177		moving to another position, so I'd applied for his job back in early August. Of course, all that
178		was before the first incident between us.

179	Q:	And when this group of people sat down, the conversation turned to you?
180		
181	A:	Not at first, according to Amanda. The children she was with had finished eating and were
182		playing nearby, so she just sat there having a cup of coffee. She wasn't trying to listen, but
183		they were engrossed in their conversation over there at the other table. It seemed like they
184		didn't notice her. She said that at first they were just talking about casual things, but then
185		someone asked about the software piracy that had taken place.
186		
187	Q:	Now, again, that was what Mr. McRaney accused you of doing that night in August?
188		
189	A:	Well, that's what he said anyhow. I don't believe he really thought that. But to answer your
190		question, yes, there's been some theft regarding hospital software. And some of it was tied
191		in with patients' records, which is of course a potential liability for the hospital.
192		
193	Q:	And Ms. Rinehart began to discuss that at the table?
194		
195	A:	Yes. Amanda said she began to talk about some serious breaches in hospital protocol
196		recently, and reiterated what she'd told me that day in her office—that she wanted
197		everybody to insist that employees be where they were supposed to be, and do what they
198		were supposed to do. She wanted increased vigilance all around the premises. And that's
199		when Charles spoke up and said what he did.
200		
201	Q:	What was that?
202		
203	A:	He broke in and said that in his opinion, management was already doing that—being as
204		vigilant as they possibly could—but that the staff had to cooperate, too. He said there were
205		some "rogue" elements loose that frustrated any attempts to control this problem.
206		
207	Q:	Who do you understand him to be referring to?
208		
209	A:	Me, of course. Amanda did too. Because as soon as she heard him say that, she sat up and
210		paid close attention. There were a few more exchanges, then Charles broke in again and
211		said something about the staff needing to be controlled. It seemed like he was making a
212		concerted effort to turn the conversation towards me.
213		
214	Q:	At what point did Ms. Stevenson begin to record the conversation?
215		
216	A:	Right then. I'd told her to let me know if anyone said anything about me at the picnic, so
217		she took out her phone and began to capture it on video. She was discreet, but she said they
218		were so involved in the conversation over there that no one paid her any mind.
219		
220	Q:	What did Mr. McRaney go on to say?
221		
222	A:	Well, as you'll be able to see on the video, he swings the conversation back around to
223		the staff. Then he says something like: "The breaches in protocol we've had around our
224		department are the very reason I don't think Grace Garrett should have that promotion."
225		
226	Q:	He was referring to the Assistant Coding Administrator job you'd applied for?
227		
228	A:	Yes.
229		
230	Q:	But what did he mean by breaches of protocol around your department? Why would he say
231		that?
232		
233	A:	Well, other than that night in August, there were times when I wasn't always in my
234		office when I was supposed to be—as far as he's concerned, that is. From time to time,
235		I was down at Sarah Wright's office. Anyhow, he reprimanded me twice for finding out
236		passwords to use certain computer programs that I needed. The formal procedure I was
237		supposed to follow was for me to request the data from the person with authority over it.
238		But that always takes such a long time—if it ever gets done at all—that I admit to taking

| 239 | | some shortcuts. I'd just go during lunch and get the data I needed from whatever office |

239   some shortcuts. I'd just go during lunch and get the data I needed from whatever office
240   had it. I got the janitorial staff to let me into the main Coding Office one day. But all that
241   was for efficiency's sake, you understand. I was doing it for the Hospital—as part of my
242   job. They should've thanked me, not reprimanded me, for such a thing.
243

244   Q: What exactly did Mr. McRaney say in that regard?
245

246   A: I have it written down. I transcribed it from the video, which you can see for yourself.
247   But here's what he said: "Not only does Grace take liberties with other people's
248   computers, equipment, and data, she's grossly insubordinate about it. I've had to
249   reprimand her time and again. And on top of that, she wanders about into other people's
250   offices and just helps herself to sensitive information. Any rules about procedure are
251   wasted on her."
252

253   Q: And he was talking to whom when he said this?
254

255   A: He was talking to everybody at the table, from what it looks like. The worse thing is that he
256   knows I was only doing my job. That place resists anyone that's just trying to get the work
257   done. When you ask for information, it's slow at best, and never delivered at worst. I was
258   even commended, privately, for my work product by Ms. Rinehart at one point. But Charles
259   presented things as though I was just running around the halls, playing and snooping and
260   gossiping.
261

262   Q: What was their response?
263

264   A: Well, nothing, because as soon as he said that, some guy came into the tent with a
265   microphone and started to talk about a raffle they were having. I couldn't really make it out,
266   but there's a few minutes lull while they listen to him. Then the guy leaves, and everybody
267   there starts to get up from the table. I guess they were going out to the raffle that was about
268   to start.
269

270   Q: Everybody?
271

272   A: Yes. From their table and from all of the other tables, too. They all get up and take their
273   plates and things from the table and step towards the front of the tent. You can see
274   Rosemary and Thomas walk away, but the others stop when Robert Jackson and his
275   secretary, Sarah Wright, walk up.
276

277   Q: Is Jackson on the Committee for Advancements?
278

279   A: No, and of course Sarah isn't either. She's Charles' secretary and Robert's.
280

281   Q: Does McRaney continue talking?
282

283   A: Yes, even with people milling around to leave the tent, passing by him, he kept talking.
284

285   Q: What did he say?
286

287   A: He said—I'll read it to you. I have it transcribed, too: "And another thing, Grace has got
288   so many personal problems. She's a terribly neglectful mother, which is probably why her
289   ex-husband's fighting her for custody, if you ask me. She doesn't take the time to raise them,
290   which is a character issue. Plus that whole incident on the news and in the papers about her
291   violent divorce proceeding was just so unseemly. She's a total nightmare for anyone involved
292   with her."
293

294   Q: Does the conversation about you end there?
295

296   A: Apparently. But that last part—I just couldn't believe it when I heard that. I mean, as I've
297   told you—he's complained and yelled about me having to go take care of my children, and
298   for having to go to custody hearings which he knows I've been deeply involved with. He's

299 even complained to Sarah and Rosemary that I was on "never-ending maternity leave." It
300 was just a downright lie.
301
302 Q: And when he referred to the "violent divorce proceedings" in the news, he was referring
303   to—
304
305 A: Yes. As you know, my ex-husband had a violent outburst in court one day, aimed at me. He
306   had to be restrained by the officers there. He made some threats directed at the judge. The
307   whole thing was in the papers and I was interviewed on the local news. Somehow, the story
308   got picked up by one of the newswires and made it into some out-of-town media markets.
309   The next week, when we had another hearing, the cameras showed up again— I guess
310   in hopes that my ex-husband would make another scene—but nothing happened and the
311   follow-up story was only carried by one local station.
312
313 Q: Back to the video. Did anyone respond to what Mr. McRaney had to say about you?
314
315 A: I can't tell. Not from the video. All I know is that I didn't get the job. I wasn't told why, but
316   they hired somebody from outside.
317
318 Q: And you believe that was the direct cause of what Mr. McRaney said?
319
320 A: I'm sure of it. Amanda says I was the top candidate until then, and the person they
321   eventually hired hadn't even been on the short list before.
322
323 Q: All right. Now show me the video.
324
325 [Ms. Garrett plays the aforementioned video file for Mr. Sheffield].
326
327 Q: Thank you. That's all I need from you at present. End of Interview.10:40 A.M.
328
329
330 Clayton Marshall
331 Stenographer

OPEN UNIVERSE MEMORANDUM

To: New Associate
From: Mitchell Thomas
Re: Charles McRaney-M.P. Matter
Date: Today, YEAR

Today, I met with Charles McRaney, a Coding Supervisor with Twin Oaks Hospital. Mr. McRaney and his employer were co-defendants in a civil action for intentional infliction of emotional distress. The action was brought here in Overland Park with regard to an incident in the Hospital's records office back in August. The co-defendants moved for summary judgment, and the motion was granted. However, Mr. McRaney had to defend himself by securing our firm as separate counsel, and the whole process resulted in his payment of considerable legal fees.

I've attached the transcript of the client interview with Mr. McRaney. He believes he was unjustly targeted by a lawsuit when he was only doing his job, a fact he says Ms. Garrett knew. At this point, I want you to focus on whether Mr. McRaney has a claim for malicious prosecution. Assume damages in the form of the legal fees and other ancillary costs.

Provide me with a memo on this matter.

1 Client Interview: Charles McRaney, Potential Malicious Prosecution claim (File No. 190828ST)
2
3 Mitchell Thomas: This is a client interview with Charles McRaney, at the Overland Park, Kansas
4 office of Thomas, Bradley and Coe. The date is Today, YEAR. It's 10:00 A.M. Present are myself,
5 Mitchell Thomas – Mr. McRaney, our client – and our stenographer, Kate Grisham.
6
7 Q: Mr. McRaney, although our firm has represented you before, I'll be asking you to repeat
8   some information just so we can have it in the transcript for this separate matter.
9   All right?
10
11 A: Okay.
12
13 Q: Would you state your full name, age, and address?
14
15 A: Charles Baylor McRaney, fifty-five. I live at 273 West High Street, Overland Park,
16   Kansas.
17
18 Q: And you're employed by Twin Oaks Hospital here in town?
19
20 A: Yes.
21
22 Q: You've been a Coding Supervisor at Twin Oaks for how long?
23
24 A: About fifteen years.
25
26 Q: Tell me more about that position. What exactly is a "Coding Supervisor"?
27
28 A: Well, I'm in charge of the hospital's coding practice and oversee a staff of about ten people.
29   We make sure the correct pre-assigned code is associated with each procedure performed at
30   the hospital, as well as with all therapies, prescriptions and the like, so that the bills can
31   be submitted for payment.
32
33 Q: So for insurance purposes, Medicare, Medicaid—that kind of thing, right?
34
35 A: Yes.
36
37 Q: And Ms. Garrett is one of the employees under your supervision?
38
39 A: She was. She was a Medical Records Coordinator.
40
41 Q: She resigned?
42
43 A: Last week.
44
45 Q: And her role as a records coordinator was entering codes on the records, is that a fair
46   description of her job?
47
48 A: Yes.
49
50 Q: And how long had she been an employee at Twin Oaks? Before her resignation, that is.
51
52 A: About a year.
53
54 Q: What kind of working relationship did you have?
55
56 A: It was pretty standard for the first few months. Then her personal life began to affect her
57   work.
58
59 Q: What do you mean?
60

61	A:	She's been involved in a long, drawn-out custody battle with her ex-husband over her
62		two sons. It caused her to miss a good deal of work—too much in my opinion. She went
63		to what seemed an endless number of hearings and legal conferences. But she also left
64		from time to time because she'd say she was a single parent and that she was the only
65		one to take care of her boys. The whole business has been in the newspapers and on the
66		T.V. The proceedings have gotten out of hand—threats and outbursts and just all kinds
67		of unseemly behavior. It reflects poorly on the hospital every time they say where she
68		works.
69		
70	Q:	Had you spoken to Ms. Garrett about this?
71		
72	A:	Yes, of course. As her supervisor, I let it be known that she had to do her job, regardless of
73		what else was going on in her life.
74		
75	Q:	And did she?
76		
77	A:	For the most part. For a while, she worked overtime when she could find someone to look
78		after her children. But then I found out she was also working heavily as a volunteer for
79		a political campaign that's going on right now. So she managed to find the time for the
80		campaign. That's what made me suspicious of her excuses. She seemed to have a lot of
81		extenuating circumstances whenever it fit her schedule.
82		
83	Q:	Did you have any major arguments?
84		
85	A:	Yes. Some. She raised her voice to me and I raised mine to her. I won't accept
86		insubordination. She wandered around the hospital and let herself into people's offices
87		to get files and things—ones that she said she needed—without going through the file
88		request protocol that I'd set up. She even got a password once to somebody else's computer
89		so she could get some information she said she needed. So we had some pretty heated
90		exchanges.
91		
92	Q:	Let's get to the matter at hand. Ms. Garrett instituted a civil action against you personally
93		for intentional infliction of emotional distress based on events that transpired on the twelfth
94		of August this year. The action was filed soon thereafter. Of course, our firm represented
95		you, and the district court granted our motion for summary judgment.
96		
97	A:	That's right.
98		
99	Q:	Just to get this into the interview transcript, I'll relate a basic narrative of the events of
100		August 12 as you told them to me. This will serve to remind you of what transpired, in case
101		something has bearing on the new matter that you've brought to us today.
102		
103	A:	All right.
104		
105	Q:	On that night, around 6:00 p.m., you stopped by the records office to leave a file in the
106		file room. You heard a noise in the adjoining office, that of the secretary Sarah Wright.
107		This surprised you, as you'd thought everyone had left for the day. You entered Ms.
108		Wright's office to find Ms. Garrett sitting at the computer. She had not received overtime
109		permission from you and was downloading something to a flash drive. Ms. Garrett
110		seemed startled. You asked what she was doing, and she said she was getting some files
111		that you had not forwarded to her. Confused, you demanded she surrender the flash
112		drive, suspecting that she might be pirating software and hospital data, an occurrence
113		that had happened twice of late there at the hospital. You were particularly concerned
114		because Ms. Garrett was on the only computer that the hospital sells a software package
115		through—one that you yourself had designed and the hospital has the rights to. You
116		called Mr. Robert Jackson, your assistant supervisor, to assist you, and the two of you
117		stood at either door to the office. Ms. Garrett refused to give you the flash drive, and
118		answered that she had permission from Ms. Wright to be where she was. You called
119		security. You did not let Ms. Garrett leave the office, telling her that she would have to
120		explain herself to the security officers and to the police, too, if it came to that. She said

121 that she had to pick up her sons at school, but as it was after 6:00 p.m., and given the
122 circumstances, you did not believe her. You did not let her use the phone because she
123 was acting irrationally and abusive and you thought it best to let security handle the
124 situation. When they arrived at 6:30 p.m., you turned the matter over to them and said
125 that you would need a report as to their findings. You also called the police. Is that about
126 it, from your side of things?
127
128 A: That's about it.
129
130 Q: Now. You later found out that Ms. Garrett had a panic attack while driving to pick up her
131 sons. She went to the hospital by way of an ambulance and has been under treatment since
132 that time for what she says is a new, uncontrollable anxiety associated with driving.
133
134 A: That's what she says, yes.
135
136 Q: Had you known of Ms. Garrett's condition before?
137
138 A: You mean her medical condition? The panic attacks?
139
140 Q: That's what I'm referring to, yes.
141
142 A: Absolutely not. I had no idea about that. I knew about her divorce and the custody battle,
143 just like I told you. Everybody who reads the news or watches T.V. knows about that. But
144 that's all I knew.
145
146 Q: Now I want to ask you to repeat for this transcript the immediate chronological context
147 within which the confrontation in the office took place.
148
149 A: You mean the software and records thefts that had been going on?
150
151 Q: Yes. Repeat that for the record.
152
153 A: Well, in the three week period prior to that night when I found Grace in the records office,
154 we'd twice suffered some thefts of expensive software. Someone had gotten into various
155 systems and downloaded files. Now that's a big deal, not only because our software was
156 stolen, but because patients' private records had been compromised. We could face liability
157 over that. So Ms. Rinehart—
158
159 Q: She's the Hospital Administrator at Twin Oaks. Correct?
160
161 A: Yes, that's right. She'd called a meeting with me and Robert Jackson the very week before
162 I found Grace in the office. Ms. Rinehart had told us how serious all this was, and said that
163 we had to find out what happened and stop it. She was angry, and she let me know that I
164 would be personally accountable for any further thefts that took place. She said she was
165 vesting Robert and me with the authority to police this matter and to stop any thefts—stop
166 them, by whatever means it took to do so.
167
168 Q; What did you do after that meeting?
169
170 Q: I called my own meeting—a meeting of the coding coordinators and our associated staff.
171 I told them the seriousness of the situation. I said that I was going to be extra vigilant
172 about things from now on and that no one was to be anywhere at any time that he or
173 she wasn't supposed to be. All requests were to go through standard protocols, without
174 exception.
175
176 Q: So later that week, when you saw Ms. Garrett in Ms. Wright's office—
177
178 A: I did just what I was told to do by Ms. Rinehart. I stopped her. I acted just as I was told.
179
180 Q: Now, let's get to the new events that transpired after that night in the office.

27

181	A:	Well, the security guard wrote up his report and gave it to me and Ms. Rinehart the next
182		day. When we reviewed the flash drive, we didn't find any of the software or data. It was
183		just innocuous stuff that related to some files Grace had been after for a while. I'd forgotten
184		she'd wanted them. Anyhow, we called her into the office and apologized. Ms. Rinehart told
185		her that it was she who had told me to be so vigilant about things because of the thefts—
186		and though I could be over-zealous at times—still, it was her doing and she was responsible.
187		She said that everyone was under a lot of pressure and worry over the situation, and that
188		things tended to get out of hand at such times. She wrote Grace a hand-written apology on
189		top of that, from the both of us, about how sorry she was for things escalating to the degree
190		that they had. She even offered her the rest of the week off, considering the strain she
191		must've been put through.
192		
193	Q:	And Ms. Garrett's response?
194		
195	A:	She didn't have a response. She just sat there, stone-faced. She wouldn't take the rest of the
196		week off, she said, and then simply nodded and got up and left.
197		
198	Q:	What happened then?
199		
200	A:	As soon as we walked out of that office, things were clear. Grace wouldn't speak to me. Then,
201		the very next day, as I was leaving for work, she waited by the door leading to the staff
202		parking lot. Out of the blue, she said she was going to make sure I paid for this. She didn't
203		care about the apology she was given. She said she didn't accept it and that she was going to
204		get even with me for what happened.
205		
206	Q:	What did you say to that?
207		
208	A:	I said, "You know why I kept you there. I told you in the meeting about that stuff being
209		stolen and how I was serious about stopping it from happening again. What was I supposed
210		to think with you in Sarah's office like that?"
211		
212	Q:	What did she say in return?
213		
214	A:	She said she hadn't known I'd been given this so-called "police power"—that I hadn't told
215		them that in the meeting. She said nobody knew but me, and accused me of hiding the fact
216		so that I could spring it on her like I did. She said Robert and I were just getting her back
217		for having to take off so much time for her children. She also said that I knew she'd been
218		asking about those files for two months and that I'd said they were in the main records office
219		and that I'd get them for her.
220		
221	Q:	Had you said that?
222		
223	A:	I might have. I don't remember. I'm in charge of ten people who come to me with
224		questions and requests all day long. That's why procedures and protocols are important—
225		to keep track of things. But she ignores protocols. I told her then and there that was why
226		she couldn't just go around in people's offices, helping herself to things. She should've
227		asked my permission. Plus, I'd warned them all about taking overtime without checking
228		with me first.
229		
230	Q:	And with regard to overtime, she quoted your own past dealings to you, didn't she?
231		
232	A:	Yes. She said, "You know you always give me overtime. You give it to me whether I ask you
233		for it before or when I tell you about it after the fact. You've never refused me overtime. In
234		fact, you insisted I take it to make up for the times I had to be away."
235		
236	Q:	What was your answer?
237		
238	A:	That I'd changed all that in the meeting. I'd put them on notice at the meeting. Regardless
239		of the past, the new procedure was "no overtime without express prior permission."
240		

241 Q: What next?

242

243 A: Well, then she started yelling. Said I wouldn't even let her call about her children. Said I
244   knew that they were in danger—that her husband had threatened to steal them—and I
245   wouldn't even let her call.

246

247 Q: Did you know that in fact?

248

249 A: No. I knew she and her husband behaved violently towards each other—that's in the paper
250   and on the news. I knew he'd threatened her and I think she might've even threatened him.
251   But the thing is, I explained to her that I'd been on the spot that night. Ms. Rinehart had
252   said I would be personally responsible if any more thefts occurred out of my department—
253   and there Grace had been, in that office—wouldn't give me the flash drive or explain
254   herself—yelling and carrying on. Security was on the way. It was nearly 6:30 at night and
255   she was talking about her children still being at school? I told her that I had no idea what
256   she was talking about. I thought it best just to let security handle it. They'd do it better
257   than me, since she was so furious. I didn't have a choice.

258

259 Q: What happened then?

260

261 A: Then she really got mad. She said she was going to sue me. She said she'd be satisfied
262   even if she didn't get a thing out of it, as long as it cost me an arm and a leg and got me
263   called up to Ms. Rinehart's office for harassing people. She said she wanted me to lose my
264   job over it.

265

266 Q: Anything else?

267

268 A: She said, "If you have any sense at all, you'll pay my lawyer whatever he asks." Then she
269   walked off.

270

271 Q: With regard to the intentional infliction of emotional distress claim, what surprised you
272   most about the complaint prepared by Ms. Garrett's legal counsel?

273

274 A: The most? That she said I knew her husband had threatened to steal her children. And
275   that I hadn't said anything in the meeting about seeking prior permission for overtime.
276   She also said I knew she was seeing a doctor about her medical condition—the panic
277   attacks.

278

279 Q: Can you directly disprove any of that, with anything other than your denial?

280

281 A: Well, there's a transcript of the meeting that I called. I had my secretary transcribe it and
282   give it to every one of the people there. It shows Grace was in attendance, and it clearly
283   shows that I said prior permission was required for overtime. I don't know if she told
284   her attorney everything or held something back, but what they said in the complaint is
285   contradicted by that transcription. On top of that, you remember that when you deposed
286   her, she had to admit she couldn't remember telling me about the panic attacks. I can't
287   directly disprove her accusation that I knew about her husband's threats regarding the
288   children, but I swear I didn't know.

289

290 Q: And for the record, we referenced that transcription in our answer to the complaint. Now,
291   Mr. McRaney, is there anything else you want to add?

292

293 A: No. Except that this whole business has cost me a lot of money and grief, just like she said it
294   would.

295

296 Mr. Thomas: Thank you. That's all I need from you at present. End of Interview.10:40 A.M.

297

298 Kate Grisham
299 Stenographer

Assignment 5

_____

CLIENT LETTERS

Sheffield and Major
190 Seville Place
Kansas City, Kansas 64111
Telephone: 816-900-4220
Facsimile: 816-900-4221
Email:shef@sheffieldandmajor.com

From: William Sheffield
To: Drafting Attorney
Re: Grace Garrett Matter
Date: Today, YEAR.

Draft a client letter to Grace Garrett apprising her of her position with regard to a potential qualified privilege defense to her claim of defamation against Charles McRaney.

When suggesting a course of action for Ms. Garrett to take, consider the client's position under the law as you have related it to me in your interoffice memorandum on the matter.

FDE/ws

Thomas, Bradley and Coe
Attorneys at Law
Suite 719 C
Trust Bank Tower
Overland Park, Kansas 64111
Telephone: 816-555-0834
Facsimile: 816-555-9812
Email: mt@tbclawfirm.com

From: Mitchell Thomas
To: Drafting Attorney
Re: Charles McRaney Matter
Date: Today, YEAR.

Draft a client letter to Charles McRaney apprising him of his position with regard to a potential malicious prosecution claim against Grace Garrett.

When suggesting a course of action for Mr. McRaney to take, consider the client's position under the law as you have related it to me in your interoffice memorandum on the matter.

SMV/lr

Assignment 6

PLEADINGS: FCA

Sheffield and Major
190 Seville Place
Kansas City, Kansas 64111
Telephone: 816-900-4220
Facsimile: 816-900-4221
Email: shef@sheffieldandmajor.com

INTEROFFICE MEMORANDUM

From: William L. Sheffield
To: Associate
Date: August 20, YR-1
Re: Grace Garrett

As you recall, Grace Garrett is a twenty-nine-year-old Medical Records Specialist with Twin Oaks Hospital in Overland Park, Kansas. She came to our office with questions about various claims, the most complex involving an employment matter that she believes concerns Medicare fraud. Ms. Garrett has been employed at the hospital for about a year.

As one of her responsibilities, Ms. Garrett encodes procedures and treatments performed at the hospital for billing purposes. When a hospital prepares to seek reimbursement for procedures or treatments performed, that event is "coded" according to a standardized classification system used throughout the country. The system ensures that all of those who use the system—hospitals, doctors, insurers—are using the same language to refer to the same things.

At a staff meeting on June 3 of this year, Ms. Garrett alerted her superiors to a potential error in coding procedures. Present at the meeting were: Ms. Garrett; nine other Records Specialists; Mr. Charles McRaney, the Records Supervisor; and Ms. Rosemary Rinehart, the Hospital Administrator. Some of Ms. Garrett's colleagues had been confused as to why Mr. McRaney had ordered them to code cases of "basic pneumonia" as "severe pneumococcal pneumonia," a more serious respiratory disease. According to Ms. Garrett, the choice was potentially incorrect based on the medical records. Ms. Rinehart instructed Mr. McRaney to look into the matter that Ms. Garrett brought up. No more was said to her, and the coding practices continued as they were.

On July 25 of this year, while reviewing some files, Ms. Garrett learned that one of the hospital's former patients, Walter L. Ridley, on March 1, YR-1, had been treated for basic pneumonia. The code used on the bill submitted to Medicare for reimbursement (Hospital I.D. #101010-ABC on March 22, YR-1) was for the severe pneumococcal pneumonia, a serious respiratory infection, which has the same code that was questioned back in the spring.

Throughout the month of August, Ms. Garrett looked further into the matter and discovered that the procedures were coded the same way in the files of another fourteen patients, all residents of the nearby retirement facility, River Crest Retirement Facility, where Mr. Ridley also lived. The difference in reimbursement for the hospital between the two codes, per case, is $30,000, totaling $450,000. The other claims were dated according to the following schedule:

I.D. #101010-DEF: February 13, YR-1;
I.D. #101010-CAD: February 14, YR-1;
I.D. #101010-DED: March 1, YR-1;
I.D. #101010-ERT: March 3, YR-1;
I.D. #101010-SSV: March 10, YR-1;
I.D. #101010-MDF: March 14, YR-1;
I.D. #101010-WWP: March 16, YR-1;
I.D. #101010-GHF: March 20, YR-1;
I.D. #101010-MMM: March 22, YR-1;
I.D. #101010-REW: March 22, YR-1;
I.D. #101010-WEH: April 2, YR-1;
I.D. #101010-PKV: April 18, YR-1;
I.D. #101010-ZQP: May 10, YR-1;
I.D. #101010-JZX: May 10, YR-1.

The above listed fourteen claims involving River Crest patients were filed collectively on June 16, YR-1.

Further investigation showed that other elderly patients with the same kind of respiratory ailment, but not residents of the nearby retirement home, were coded as basic pneumonia. Those cases were identified as follows: I.D. #101000-DSK: April 10, YR-1; I.D. #101000-FCD: May 13, YR-1.

Ms. Garrett believes that Twin Oaks Hospital, Inc., through its employees, Mr. McRaney and Ms. Rinehart, has knowingly coded these procedures at a rate higher than warranted by the facts, resulting in unjust reimbursement for the hospital.

We intend to pursue a claim under the federal False Claims Act, 31 U.S.C. § 3729(a)(1) et seq. Look into this matter, acquainting yourself with the facts necessary to file a valid complaint using the attached case, *United States ex rel. Morton v. A Plus Benefits, Inc.,* 139 F. App'x 980 (10th Cir. 2005). Draft the complaint, assuming we'll file in federal district court, using the following addresses:

Grace A. Garrett: 2394 McAllister Boulevard, Overland Park, Johnson County, Kansas, 56789

Twin Oaks Hospital, Inc.: 1510 Riparian Way, Overland Park, Johnson County, Kansas 56788

Gentry, Steyn, and Hoffman
Attorneys at Law
567 Harrison Place South
Overland Park, Kansas 64111
Telephone: 816-555-4312
Facsimile: 816-555-2111
Email: gentry@gshlaw.com

INTEROFFICE MEMORANDUM

From: Gale Gentry
To: Associate
Date: August 20, YR-1
Re: Twin Oaks Hospital Matter

Rosemary Rinehart, the Hospital Administrator at Twin Oaks Hospital, our client, has come to this firm about a lawsuit that has been filed against the hospital. According the complaint, the following facts are alleged:

Grace Garrett is a twenty-nine-year-old Medical Records Specialist with Twin Oaks Hospital in Overland Park, Kansas. Ms. Garrett has been employed at the hospital for about a year.

As one of her responsibilities, Ms. Garrett encodes procedures and treatments performed at the hospital for billing purposes. When a hospital prepares to seek reimbursement for procedures or treatments performed, that event is "coded" according to a standardized classification system used throughout the country. The system ensures that all of those who use the system—hospitals, doctors, insurers—are using the same language to refer to the same things.

At a staff meeting on June 3 of this year, Ms. Garrett alerted her superiors to a potential error in coding procedures. Present at the meeting were: Ms. Garrett; nine other Records Specialists; Mr. Charles McRaney, the Records Supervisor; and Ms. Rosemary Rinehart, the Hospital Administrator. Some of Ms. Garrett's colleagues had been confused as to why Mr. McRaney had ordered them to code cases of "basic pneumonia" as "severe pneumococcal pneumonia," a more serious respiratory disease. According to Ms. Garrett, the choice was potentially incorrect based on the medical records. Ms. Rinehart instructed Mr. McRaney to look into the matter that Ms. Garrett brought up. No more was said to her, and the coding practices continued as they were.

On July 25 of this year, while reviewing some files, Ms. Garrett learned that one of the hospital's former patients, Walter L. Ridley, on March 1, YR-1, had been treated for basic pneumonia. The code used on the bill submitted to Medicare for reimbursement (Hospital I.D. # 101010-ABC on March 22, YR-1) was for the severe pneumococcal pneumonia, a serious respiratory infection, which has the same code that was questioned back in the spring.

Throughout the month of August, Ms. Garrett looked further into the matter and discovered that the procedures were coded the same way in the files of another fourteen patients, all residents of the nearby retirement facility, River Crest Retirement Facility, where Mr. Ridley also lived. The difference in reimbursement for the hospital between the two codes, per case, is

$30,000, totaling $450,000. The other claims were dated according to the following schedule:

I.D. #101010-DEF: February 13, YR-1;
I.D. #101010-CAD: February 14, YR-1;
I.D. #101010-DED: March 1, YR-1;
I.D. #101010-ERT: March 3, YR-1;
I.D. #101010-SSV: March 10, YR-1;
I.D. #101010-MDF: March 14, YR-1;
I.D. #101010-WWP: March 16, YR-1;
I.D. #101010-GHF: March 20, YR-1;
I.D. #101010-MMM: March 22, YR-1;
I.D. #101010-REW: March 22, YR-1;
I.D. #101010-WEH: April 2, YR-1;
I.D. #101010-PKV: April 18, YR-1;
I.D. #101010-ZQP: May 10, YR-1;
I.D. #101010-JZX: May 10, YR-1.

The above listed fourteen claims involving River Crest patients were filed collectively on June 16, YR-1.

Further investigation showed that other elderly patients with the same kind of respiratory ailment, but not residents of the nearby retirement home, were coded as basic pneumonia. Those cases were identified as follows: I.D. #101000-DSK: April 10, YR-1; I.D. #101000-FCD: May 13, YR-1.

Ms. Garrett alleges that Twin Oaks Hospital, Inc., through its employees, Mr. McRaney and Ms. Rinehart, knowingly coded these procedures at a rate higher than warranted by the facts, resulting in unjust reimbursement for the hospital.

Ms. Garrett is pursuing a claim under the federal False Claims Act, 31 U.S.C. § 3729(a)(1). The complaint is attached. Draft an answer to the complaint.

Assignment 7

BRIEF: FCA CLAIM

Sheffield and Major
190 Seville Place
Kansas City, Kansas 64111
Telephone: 816-900-4220
Facsimile: 816-900-4221
Email: shef@sheffieldandmajor.com

INTEROFFICE MEMORANDUM

From: William Sheffield
To: Associate
Date: Today, YEAR
Re: United States <u>ex rel</u>. Grace A. Garrett v. Twin Oaks Hospital, Inc.

As you are aware, Twin Oaks Hospital, Inc. has filed a Motion for Summary Judgment in the above-styled case. Ms. Garrett intends to file a Response to that Motion. Please draft a memorandum of law in opposition to the Motion for Summary Judgment.

Gentry, Steyn, and Hoffman
Attorneys at Law
567 Harrison Place South
Overland Park, Kansas 64111
Telephone: 816-555-4312
Facsimile: 816-555-2111
Email: gentry@gshlaw.com

INTEROFFICE MEMORANDUM

From: Gale Gentry
To: Associate
Re: United States <u>ex rel</u>. Grace A. Garrett v. Twin Oaks Hospital, Inc.
Date: Today, YEAR.

As you are aware, Twin Oaks Hospital, Inc. has filed a Motion for Summary Judgment in the above referenced matter. Grace Garrett intends to file a Response to that Motion.

Please draft a memorandum of law in support of the Motion for Summary Judgment.

Deposition of Grace Anne Garrett

Office of Gentry, Steyn, and Hoffman

Kansas City, Kansas, December 1, YR-1, 10:00 A.M.

After having been sworn, Grace A. Garrett testified:

Examination by Ms. Gentry:

Q: For the record, state your full name and age.

A: Grace Anne Garrett, 29.

Q: Your address?

A: 2394 McAllister Boulevard, Overland Park, Kansas.

Q: Have you ever been deposed before, Ms. Garrett?

A: No, I haven't.

Q: All right. For clarity's sake, a deposition, which you're about to give, is sworn testimony that can be used in the court proceeding you've instituted under the False Claims Act against your former employer, Twin Oaks Hospital. I'll ask you questions, then your own attorney may do the same, and so forth. The court reporter will record all this. Do you understand?

A: Yes.

Q: You came here today in response to a subpoena from the federal district court here in Kansas City, correct?

A: Yes.

Q: And you've sworn to tell the truth today?

A: Yes.

Q: Do you have any qualifications about that oath?

A: No.

Q: Are you on any medications, stimulants, or drugs, or do you have any health problems that would interfere with your testimony?

A: No.

Q: We can take a break any time you'd like. You just say so. All right?

A: Yes.

Q: If you don't understand a question, I'll rephrase it for you. Or if you didn't hear it, I'll be glad to repeat it. Just ask.

A: Okay.

Q: Now, your attorney has the right to object to something I ask, and he'll tell you whether to proceed with a response. The objection, at any rate, will go into the record for the court to decide whether the substance of the statement is admissible at trial. Okay?

A: Yes.

Q: Was there anything unclear about what I just told you?

A: No. I understand.

Q: So you can think of no reason why you cannot give full and accurate testimony here today?

A: No.

Q: All right then. Ms. Garrett, are you currently employed?

A: No. As you're aware, I left my job as a Medical Records Specialist at Twin Oaks back in October—the 21st, to be exact—and I haven't found employment as of yet.

Q: What exactly does a Medical Records Specialist do?

A: Well, we're in charge of assigning payment codes to procedures and treatments performed at the Hospital. For reimbursement purposes.

Q: I'm sorry. Explain that: "Payment codes for reimbursement purposes."

A: Oh. Well, when someone's treated at the Hospital—undergoes surgery, let's say—or undergoes some kind of diagnostic procedure or is treated for some ailment—that event is "coded," according to the category of treatment codes on the ICD-9-CM, or one of the other appropriate coding systems, and then sent in to the patient's insurer for payment. So basically I'm one of—or I was one of—the people who review medical records, physicians' notes, physicians' consults, etc., to determine the proper code to assign to the proper procedure or treatment.

59	Q:	You'll have to explain that too, I'm afraid. The ICD-9-CM?
60	A:	It's just a universal classification system used by American health care providers. It's
61		overseen by NCHS and—
62	Q:	NCHS?
63	A:	The National Center for Health Services—they oversee it, along with the Medicare/Medicaid
64		Center. Basically, the system just ensures that all of those who employ it—hospitals,
65		doctors, insurers—are using the same language to refer to the same things. There are other
66		applicable coding systems, but the main thing is that these classifications provide a unified
67		system for health care providers.
68	Q:	How long had you held that position, prior to your voluntary resignation from—
69	Mr. Sheffield:	Objection. She didn't admit that.
70	Ms. Gentry:	She just said she left her job a few minutes ago. I was only—
71	Mr. Sheffield:	She didn't say she resigned. She left, in her view, out of necessity, due to her
72		former employer's treatment of her. She said nothing about resigning voluntarily.
73		Opposing counsel knows we've preserved that claim against her client.
74	Ms. Gentry:	I'll rephrase the question. Ms. Garrett, when you left Twin Oaks, how long had
75		you worked there?
76	A:	About a year. Before that, I'd worked for about a year at St. Michael's Hospital here in town,
77		in a similar capacity.
78	Q:	So you trained for this position in school?
79	A:	No, actually I have a journalism degree. I'd meant to work in that field, but got married
80		right out of college and had my first son the next year. When my ex-husband and I moved
81		here, I fell into this line of work, as there were openings in the area and the hours were
82		better.
83	Q:	You have no training in the medical records field then?
84	A:	In fact, I do. I had on-the-job training at first, but I also completed an AHIMA—that's
85		American Health Information Management Association—certificate program at a local
86		community college. So that makes two years working in the records field before my
87		certification and two years afterwards.
88	Q:	And how many people work as Medical Records Specialists at Twin Oaks?
89	A:	Ten at my level, including me. Then there's Charles McRaney, the Records Supervisor, and
90		until not long ago, Robert Jackson, was his assistant. He's now left that position for another
91		one with the Hospital. At least that's my understanding about the current arrangements.
92		Since I'm not there any longer, I can't say for sure.
93	Q:	All right, now let me ask you about your journalism degree that you just mentioned. Am
94		I correct in saying that you employed those skills as part of Stuart Chamberlain's campaign
95		for U.S. Congress?
96	A:	That's right.
97	Q:	You worked in what capacity for his campaign?
98	A:	I volunteered. I worked for his media committee.
99	Q:	You were the vice-chair of that committee, isn't that right, Ms. Garrett?
100	A:	I was.
101	Q:	And you prepared press releases, coordinated media events for him, that kind of thing?
102	A:	Yes.
103	Q:	You attended his press conferences, rallies, and all campaign events, didn't you?
104	A:	When they didn't conflict with my work schedule, of course. Or interfere with my family
105		obligations.
106	Q:	But you attended his press conference and rally at River Crest Retirement Community on
107		July 25th, did you not?
108	A:	Yes. I was there.
109	Q:	And in your capacity as a member of his campaign team, correct?
110	A:	Of course.
111	Q:	And the purpose of Mr. Chamberlain's appearance there at River Crest?
112	A:	It was because of a plank in his campaign platform—to help the elderly citizens of this
113		district.
114	Q:	All right. Now, you also recall, Ms. Garrett, that Mr. Chamberlain's particular reason for
115		appearing at the retirement community that day was because of some trouble he said that
116		one of the retirees there—a Mr. Walter Ridley—was having with his health care?
117	A:	Yes.

118	Q:	And you recall that Mr. Chamberlain learned of this because of a letter he'd received from
119		Mr. Ridley?
120	A:	Yes.
121	Q:	I'm now handing the witness a document supplied to me by my client, Twin Oaks Hospital.
122		The court reporter will please designate it Deposition Exhibit A. Do you recognize that
123		document, Ms. Garrett?
124	A:	Yes. It's a press release regarding Mr. Chamberlain's appearance at the retirement
125		community.
126	Q:	Who prepared that release, Ms. Garrett?
127	A:	I did.
128	Q:	And if you will, please take a moment and familiarize yourself with the contents of that
129		release.
130		
131		(MS. GARRETT READS THE DOCUMENT.)
132		
133	Q:	You've had a chance to read the press release completely, Ms. Garrett?
134	A:	Yes.
135	Q:	Good, now please read aloud the third through the fifth paragraphs of that release.
136	A:	The third through the fifth?
137	Q:	Yes, if you would.
138	A:	"As an example of the trying circumstances that many of these elderly retirees face,
139		Candidate Chamberlain brought up a member of the audience, Walter L. Ridley.
140		Mr. Ridley, 85, has gone through a harrowing experience regarding payment under his
141		Medicare coverage. 'Walter has gone back and forth with a local hospital that has submitted
142		his claims for payment to Medicare,' said Chamberlain, 'only to have many rejected
143		outright, re-submitted, and rejected again. One of his problems—involving a respiratory
144		matter last spring—was recently resolved and the payment made—miraculously—with no
145		explanation. Of course, you can imagine the kind of stress that puts on someone like Walter
146		and his family, who never know from one minute to the next whether they're going to be
147		faced with a huge hospital bill over something they thought was covered.' Chamberlain went
148		on to say that Mr. Ridley has friends there at River Crest with similar bad experiences, as
149		respiratory ailments are common to people his age. They have all gone through the same
150		ordeal—if their problem is resolved at all, it's without explanation. 'I'm going to look into
151		this myself,' said Chamberlain. 'Coverage should be clear when it comes to your health.
152		It shouldn't be a roulette wheel or a mystery movie. I'm going to talk to these people, so
153		that we can get to the bottom of at least one of these absurd bureaucratic dilemmas facing
154		seniors today.'"
155	Q:	Thank you, Ms. Garrett. That's enough. Now, did you prepare that release on the date of the
156		press event, July 25th?
157	A:	Yes, I prepared it for immediate release.
158	Q:	And the press was in fact in attendance that day, were they not? Reporters for the major
159		state and local daily newspapers and the television stations?
160	A:	That was the point.
161	Q:	So they were?
162	A:	Yes, they were.
163	Q:	And stories quoting this language you just read appeared in the media coverage following
164		this event, did they not?
165	A:	Yes, they did.
166	Q:	To your knowledge, Ms. Garrett, did Mr. Chamberlain follow through on his campaign
167		promise—to talk to Mr. Ridley's friends with similar problems?
168	A:	I believe he did. I know he stayed around that day at the retirement community for that
169		purpose. I'm not privy to any more information than that.
170	Q:	But you're confirming that to your knowledge he did begin, on that very day, to conduct his
171		own investigation into the matters that are the subject of that press release?
172	A:	He followed through on what he said.
173	Q:	Now then, as that's the case, let's turn to your claim under the FCA—that's the "False
174		Claims Act," as you know. Ms. Garrett, in your Complaint, you state in paragraph #19 that
175		Twin Oaks Hospital submitted a Medicare claim regarding Walter L. Ridley of Overland
176		Park, Kansas' treatment for severe pneumococcal pneumonia, a serious respiratory

177 infection, when in fact the Hospital knew that the treatment for Mr. Ridley's ailment
178 indicated only a more basic, milder form of pneumonia. That's a fair characterization of
179 the claim?
180 A: Yes.
181 Q: And you go on, in paragraphs #20 through #33 to list another fourteen incidents that you
182 say are factually false claims for payment with regard to fourteen other individuals in
183 similar circumstances, isn't that so?
184 A: Yes, that's what it says.
185 Q: Now, Ms. Garrett, you also claim in paragraph #15 that you expanded your investigation
186 into what you call the fraudulent coding practices at the Hospital, correct?
187 A: Yes.
188 Q: But is it not so, Ms. Garrett, that you learned of Mr. Ridley's problems with regard to his
189 Medicare coverage from the media event that day on July 25th, the one brought to the
190 world's attention by Mr. Chamberlain?
191 A: No, not at all. My allegations are based on facts I discovered through my own
192 investigation and industry—over an entire month-long period—one that was resisted by
193 the Hospital, if I might add. Mr. Chamberlain's statements that day were vague. They
194 didn't identify the problem or the hospital that he was referring to, or any of the other
195 parties. He only aroused my curiosity about a problem I'd already noticed at work. He
196 was at most an inspiration for me to take the initiative that I did. The initiative itself
197 was all mine.
198 Q: You admit that the other allegations, besides those related to Mr. Ridley, are of the exact
199 same nature as his?
200 Mr. Sheffield: That's been asked and answered.
201 Ms. Gentry: This is not the same question. The first related to how Ms. Garrett learned of
202 her information. I'm now asking whether the claim she denies as having learned
203 from Mr. Chamberlain is the same in nature as the others she lists in her com-
204 plaint. So are they of the same nature, Ms. Garrett?
205 A: They're the same kind of fraud, yes.
206 Q: And these other claims, in paragraphs #20 through #33, do they also involve residents of
207 River Crest Retirement Community?
208 A: Yes.
209 Q: So how is your purpose in this complaint not exactly the same as Mr. Chamberlain's that
210 day, Ms. Garrett?
211 A: Because he was there to help the elderly. My purpose was, and is now, to expose fraud
212 perpetrated by the Hospital.
213 Q: So you're saying Mr. Chamberlain's stated objective to get to the root of this problem and
214 to interview the parties Mr. Ridley knew and could identify is only coincidentally like
215 your claim?
216 A: I'm saying that his sincere purpose that day was larger than my objective. He couldn't have
217 found out the reason for what was happening to those individuals. It took my acquaintance
218 with the records and the system to do that.
219 Q: He put you on the trail though, didn't he?
220 A: I said earlier that he motivated my curiosity. He identified the phenomenon, but I traced
221 down its cause and what it meant.
222 Q: But Ms. Garrett, wouldn't Mr. Chamberlain's comments have led just about anyone to what
223 you claim? You just gave a technical label to what was in fact the subject and essence of his
224 press conference, isn't that so?
225 A: No. I don't see how that could possibly be so. My claim is based on knowledge gleaned from
226 the Hospital records upon which I work—worked, that is—every day.
227 Q: Now, Ms. Garrett, you contacted Mr. Christopher Heller, with Medicare's Office of
228 Investigations in Wichita, Kansas?
229 A: I did, yes.
230 Q: On what date?
231 A: July 28th, YR-1.
232 Q: And why did you do that?
233 A: Because, after Mr. Chamberlain's appearance at the retirement community, as I said,
234 my curiosity was piqued. I went back and looked to see if we had a file on Mr. Ridley, and
235 we did. While there, I saw that some of his charges were being rejected as uncovered by

236		his insurance, but then other charges were going through. And I figured that those were
237		related to something I'd seen earlier—a problem we'd had back in the spring. I thought
238		about it for a few days, then called what I believed was the Medicare fraud tip line in their
239		regional office.
240	Q:	But it wasn't the tip line, was it Ms. Garrett?
241	A:	No. Through no fault of my own, I reached another line.
242	Q:	How did that happen?
243	A:	Because after the press event and my initial inquiry, I asked a friend at work, Sarah
244		Wright—she's Charles McRaney's secretary—who you'd contact at the Medicare office if
245		you had some suspicions about all this. As it turned out, she knew a man who works for the
246		HHS Inspector General's field office.
247	Q:	For the record, you're referring to the Department of Health and Human Services, correct?
248	A:	Yes. Anyway, Sarah thought I could contact him through a confidential tip line and leave a
249		message about suspected fraud.
250	Q:	That's Mr. Heller you're referring to?
251	A:	Yes. She'd met him at a seminar and had what she thought was the number for his tip line.
252		But when I called it, someone answered. I was unsure what that meant—thinking it would
253		be a recording—but it turned out to be a temp who was unfamiliar with the phone system.
254		I explained my purpose to him, and he gave me what he said was the number I was looking
255		for. I hung up, dialed that number, and got a recording that stated I'd reached the number
256		of Christopher Heller of the Health and Human Services' Office of Investigations. I was
257		instructed to leave a message.
258	Q:	And you did so?
259	A:	Yes.
260	Q:	What did you say?
261	A:	I simply said that I was with the Chamberlain campaign's press committee, that I was
262		at the media event a few days before at River Crest Retirement Community in Overland
263		Park, and that I knew about the denial of coverage Mr. Chamberlain was referring
264		to, the one involving Mr. Ridley. I said I knew that Twin Oaks Hospital had a role in
265		that problem.
266	Q:	You didn't leave your name though, did you?
267	A:	No.
268	Q:	Or leave a number where you could be contacted?
269	A:	No. I called from a pay phone outside the Hospital.
270	Q:	And why did you do that?
271	A:	Because—that night, I was unsure of myself. I just forgot to say it. Maybe, deep down,
272		I didn't want to, until I'd learned more. I'm not in the habit of accusing my employers
273		of fraud. Who is? But when I learned more, after two weeks of work, I filed this claim.
274		My name's on it now.
275	Q:	So you filled in the rest of the information you say was so vague from the press event when
276		you left the phone message that night, calling in your capacity as a campaign worker—a
277		member of the media committee in fact—isn't that true?
278	A:	I was just making allusion to the media event to help Mr. Heller put it in context—as a
279		point of reference—so he would know what I was talking about. As I said, I didn't know
280		what to do that night. I wasn't completely sure yet whether there was any wrongdoing—not
281		until I'd completed my own investigation.
282	Q:	The line you left the message on was in fact a public line at Mr. Heller's home, wasn't it?
283	A:	I didn't know that. That's not my fault. I probably should've checked into that number before
284		I called. Apparently, Sarah was mistaken about the line she had the number for. But my
285		intention was to leave the information on the tip line.
286	Q:	Nevertheless, Mr. Heller has signed an affidavit, one that I'm asking the court reporter
287		to mark as Deposition Exhibit B, in which he states the number you called was his home
288		line—an open, public line.
289	A:	All I know is that I got inspired to investigate the matter by the press conference, did my
290		preliminary call to what I considered to be—and for all intents and purposes was in fact—a
291		tip line for Medicare fraud. I then did my own investigative work on the Hospital files and
292		made my claim. It's my understanding that the law encourages such things.
293	Q:	These files you refer to, they were open to everyone in the office, weren't they?
294	A:	To other medical Records Specialists, yes.
295	Q:	They knew of this too, then?

296	A:	Yes, but they didn't know what I found. They were perplexed, but none of them knew why
297		these claims were being coded as they were. I was the one that followed up on it and found
298		out why. When I had a clear case, I called my attorney and we filed this claim.
299	Q:	But just to be clear, the coding problems themselves were nothing you knew about from
300		direct experience? It was all after the fact, isn't that right?
301	A:	I didn't code any of the files in my Complaint myself, no. But the other Records Specialists
302		who did work on the cases asked me about the problem. As I've said, repeatedly,
303		I'm the one that brought it up in the first place. I'm the one that told Mr. McRaney
304		and Ms. Rinehart at a staff meeting that they should look into it back in June—
305		June 3rd, according to my notes. And then I'm the one that discovered why the conflict
306		was occurring.
307	Q:	You're aware that Mr. McRaney and Ms. Rinehart called the office of the Medicare
308		Intermediary—Mid-West Insurance—which answers questions about coding on Medicare's
309		behalf—after your June 3rd conversation?
310	A:	I knew they'd contacted the Intermediary at some point, but they didn't do that
311		immediately. I asked Mr. McRaney several times about it, but he didn't call for a week.
312		I doubt they'd have ever looked into it unless I'd kept after them about it.
313	Q:	Did you know that the Intermediary's office in fact confirmed the Hospital's coding practice?
314	A:	Mr. McRaney told me that that the coding practice was only provisionally approved upon
315		further review. They knew better than to think these claims were coded correctly.
316	Q:	But you don't know that they're coded incorrectly, do you?
317	A:	I'm sure that they are. They conform to the wrong definition for that code, considering the
318		gross lack of evidence in the charts. They're false claims.
319	Q:	You concede your experience and expertise in this field, compared to Mr. McRaney's,
320		is deficient by some eighteen years, correct?
321	A:	That matters? It's false regardless of, or because of, Mr. McRaney's experience.
322	Q:	But that's only a guess though, isn't it? You're just guessing that they're false, aren't you?
323		The Hospital is of the opinion that they're correct, and apparently the representative at the
324		Medicare Intermediary, whom they asked about all this, did as well.
325	A:	I'm convinced they're false and convinced that the Hospital knew them to be so.
326		They never followed through to find out whether their provisional approval from the
327		Intermediary representative would stand, and persisted in coding things the wrong way
328		thereafter.
329	Q:	Did you ever mention this to Mr. Chamberlain, whom you say inspired your
330		investigation?
331	A:	In passing.
332	Q:	Why not at length, if this was so important to him? Why would you keep this information
333		quiet until after you'd filed your claim for damages against the Hospital?
334	A:	Because I didn't want to say something before I knew what I was talking about. Also, he
335		was busy on the campaign trail. His was a special election held last November, and he was
336		all over the state at the time. I once told him at a rally in Topeka that I was looking into
337		Mr. Ridley's problem. He encouraged me to do so and said that we'd talk about it after
338		the election.
339	Q:	Ms. Garrett, weren't you reprimanded for going into other people's offices without
340		permission, and for obtaining computer passwords that were forbidden you?
341	A:	I'm zealous in doing my job. I was even complimented by Ms. Rinehart, the Hospital
342		Administrator, about my work ethic. I did obtain information I needed from the places you
343		mention, but only as a part of doing my work.
344	Q:	And not as a part of what you call your investigation?
345	A:	I might've done that, but in my view that was something I had to do to expose this
346		corruption.
347	Q:	Didn't Mr. McRaney have to call security one night for your being in the Records Office at
348		someone else's computer?
349	A:	I was cleared of all wrongdoing there, and received a formal apology from Ms. Rinehart for
350		Mr. McRaney's behavior.
351	Q:	Do you still harbor some animosity towards, Mr. McRaney?
352	A:	No more than he does towards me.
353	Q:	Considering your turbulent working relationship, why did you apply for a job to be
354		Mr. McRaney's assistant in the Records Office?

355   A: I wanted the job. I'm qualified, it pays more, and as I'm raising my children alone now,
356   I needed the income.
357   Q: So you're looking for more income, Ms. Garrett?
358   A: In any honest way I can earn it, yes, Ms. Gentry.
359   Q: No more questions.
360
361   Examination by Mr. Sheffield:
362
363   Q: Why did you conduct the first investigation, upon hearing Mr. Chamberlain's press
364   conference?
365   A: Well, it made lights go off in my head. I thought maybe I could explain why what had
366   happened to Mr. Ridley was a common occurrence for seniors, because it seemed like
367   something I'd noticed at the Hospital earlier this year. Besides that, his name—Ridley—
368   sounded familiar – like a name I'd come across associated with the earlier coding problems
369   we'd had.
370   Q: Problems when?
371   A: Back last spring. I heard some of my friends in the office—other Records Specialists—
372   discussing why they were coding certain cases in a way that Mr. McRaney instructed them
373   to, and saying that similar cases hadn't been coded that way in the past. It had caused some
374   confusion.
375   Q: Did they approach you about the problem?
376   A: Yes. The others always come to me when they're confused, since I have a reputation around
377   the office for being the most adept at coding. Besides, the rest of them are somewhat—
378   afraid—of Mr. McRaney, and knew that I would push an issue that they would let drop.
379   Q: Did you look into these suspect files?
380   A: I did. I wanted to see if I could help. Of course, Mr. McRaney was always reprimanding me
381   for not being where I should be whenever I tried to find out. But in the end, I did in fact get
382   a handle on the situation. The other Records Specialists had showed me the files they were
383   working on with these strange codes. So I checked around and then told Mr. McRaney and
384   Ms. Rinehart that I believed an error was occurring.
385   Q: When did you do this?
386   A: In a staff meeting of our group on June 3rd of this year.
387   Q: And their reaction?
388   A: Nothing, really. Except from Ms. Rinehart, who only said that she'd have Mr. McRaney look
389   into it.
390   Q: When you made your investigation into the practices, after the press conference, and after
391   you'd made your call to the tip line, what did you do exactly?
392   A: Well, in August—throughout that month, in fact—I checked these things on the computers,
393   and checked them against the coding classification. In time, I discovered the problem not
394   only with Mr. Ridley's files, but those of other River Crest residents as well. It was clear to
395   me that these cases were being coded so that the Hospital would be reimbursed at a higher
396   rate than was justified—the one that the Hospital knew was correct. The Hospital was
397   demanding that things be characterized falsely, so that they would get a better profit.
398   Q: That wasn't apparent to you immediately though, was it?
399   A: No, and it wouldn't have been to anybody. You had to have access to the files and to detect
400   the pattern of behavior. I was the only one that put together the common link—that these
401   were all River Crest residents, with respiratory problems. I also checked and saw that
402   several other elderly patients with similar problems, but not River Crest residents, had
403   been coded at the lower rate. That's what made me draw the conclusion that the Hospital
404   was billing the newly-opened River Crest patients at a higher code than the non-River
405   Crest patients. They pretended there was an epidemic of these cases, and would've
406   continued to do so had I not stepped in.
407   Q: Why do you say that the Hospital knew?
408   A: Because they've always known how to code these cases. In the past, they coded similar
409   cases the right way. You look at the two claims that were concurrent with these fifteen, but
410   involved people who weren't residents of River Crest, and you see a basic, uncomplicated
411   pneumonia classification, even though they have the same basic medical records as the
412   cases here. McRaney has held that job for years, and to pretend at this confusion does not
413   square with his experience. This case is no more complex to determine the nature of than
414   any other.

415	Q:	And with regard to your tip line message. Although you didn't leave your name when you
416		left the information on the tip line, you did leave your name when you made your required
417		"pre-filing disclosure" with the government, did you not?
418	A:	I certainly did. You helped me prepare both a very detailed narrative to the government
419		after my investigation—when we initially talked to them about this matter—as well as a
420		disclosure statement regarding the particulars of my claim just before it was put under seal.
421		So the government was not in the dark about who I was.
422	Q:	Finally, Ms. Garrett, you've had personal confrontations with Mr. McRaney throughout
423		this year?
424	A:	Yes. He was very vocal in criticizing me for taking time off during my custody battle with
425		my ex-husband. And he and his assistant, Robert Jackson, called security on me one
426		evening, barring me from leaving to get my children after school out of some trumped up
427		suspicion that I was stealing files. I suffered great traumatic distress for that. He's also
428		opposed my candidature for promotion. He sullied my name, in public places—a company
429		picnic last fall, for example—and that's led to the loss of a promotion I was seeking, which
430		was Robert Jackson's position.
431		Mr. Sheffield: No more questions.
432		
433		(End of Deposition: 11:20 a.m., December 1, YR-1.)
434		

435   Certificate of Stenographer

436 I, Bennett Shelton, certified stenographic reporter for the court, CSR No. 6543, do hereby certify
437 that I reported in Stenograph notes the foregoing proceedings, and that they have been edited by
438 me, or under my direction and the foregoing transcript contains a full, true, complete and accurate
439 transcript of the proceedings held in this matter, to the best of my knowledge. I further certify that
440 this transcript of the proceedings truly and correctly reflects the exhibits, if any, offered by the
441 respective parties.
442   In witness, I have subscribed my name on this 1st day of December, YR-1.

Bennett Shelton
Bennett Shelton

EXHIBIT A

7/25/YR-1: FOR IMMEDIATE RELEASE:

U.S. House of Representatives Candidate Stuart Chamberlain Speaks Out On Eldercare

As one of his platform issues, Stuart Chamberlain, candidate for the U.S. House of Representatives from Kansas in the upcoming special election, appeared today at a new retirement center in the Kansas City metropolitan area.

River Crest, which accommodates three hundred residents in independent, assisted-living, and nursing facilities, was the site for Candidate Chamberlain's press conference. The reason for choosing the locale was because of a letter he'd recently received from one of River Crest's residents.

"I've made it a central point of my campaign—fighting bureaucracy," said Chamberlain, "and will make it a central point of my tenure as your U.S. Representative, to tend to the many needs that face our growing senior population in this country today. As the average age of the population increases each year, we can no longer afford to turn away from their major concerns. To do so not only affects the aged, but the younger members of their families who support and care for them."

As an example of the trying circumstances that many of these elderly retirees face, Candidate Chamberlain brought up a member of the audience, Walter L. Ridley. Mr. Ridley, 85, has gone through a harrowing experience regarding payment under his Medicare coverage.

"Walter has gone back and forth with a local hospital that has submitted his claims for payment to Medicare," said Chamberlain, "only to have many rejected outright, re-submitted, and rejected again. One of his problems—involving a respiratory matter last spring—was recently resolved and the payment made—miraculously—with no explanation. Of course, you can imagine the kind of stress that puts on someone like Walter and his family, who never know from one minute to the next whether they're going to be faced with a huge hospital bill over something they thought was covered."

Chamberlain went on to say that Mr. Ridley has friends there at River Crest with similar bad experiences, as respiratory ailments are common to people his age. They have all gone through the same ordeal: if their problem is resolved at all, it's without explanation. "I'm going to look into this myself," said Chamberlain. "Coverage should be clear when it comes to your health. It shouldn't be a roulette wheel or a mystery movie. I'm going to talk to these people, so that we can get to the bottom of at least one of these absurd bureaucratic dilemmas facing seniors today."

For more information, contact:
Grace Garrett
Stuart Chamberlain, Campaign for U.S. House of Representatives: 555-111-2323

EXHIBIT B

In The
UNITED STATES DISTRICT COURT
FOR THE DISTRICT OF KANSAS

United States <u>ex rel.</u> Grace A. Garrett)
        Plaintiff,   )   Civil Action No. 10-2345-DMO
           v.   )
Twin Oaks Hospital, Inc.,   )
        Defendant.   )

AFFIDAVIT

The undersigned affiant, being first duly sworn, hereby says:

1. I hereby state that I am over the age of eighteen, suffer no legal disabilities, have personal knowledge of the facts set forth below, and am competent to testify.

2. I hereby state that I am an investigator with the Department of Health and Human Services' Office of the Inspector General in Wichita, Kansas.

3. I hereby state that as part of my employment, I am under a duty of confidentiality as to all information that I receive.

4. I hereby state that my office was aware of the press event conducted by Stuart Chamberlain on July 25, YR-1.

5. I hereby state that on July 28, YR-1, a phone message was left on my home office telephone line by an anonymous female individual, identifying herself as a member of Stuart Chamberlain's campaign press committee.

6. I hereby state that on the phone message referenced in paragraph 5, the individual referred to the events of the July 25 press conference, involving Mr. Walter Ridley. The individual named Twin Oaks Hospital as involved in the same matter.

7. I hereby state that my wife, Claire M. Heller, has access to the phone line reference in paragraphs 5 and 6 above.

8. I hereby state that my wife, Claire M. Heller, works for our office in the payroll department, in our building located at 223 S. Washington Street, Wichita, Kansas.

9. I hereby state that my wife, Claire M. Heller, is an employee of KC Payroll Services, a subcontractor to our office. All subcontractors to our office are under a contractual duty of confidentiality.

10. I hereby state that our office has not as yet instigated an investigation regarding the billing matters concerned in the Complaint referenced by this civil action number, and can state no opinion as to the direct cause of any investigation that might be initiated.

This, the 19th day of November, YR-1.
Sworn to and subscribed before me this
the 19th day of November, YR-1

Blake C. Jordache

Christopher J. Heller
Christopher J. Heller
Investigations Officer
Department of Health and
Human Services

Deposition of Charles Baylor McRaney
Office of Sheffield and Major
Overland Park, Kansas, December 7, YR-1, 10:00 A.M.

1		Deposition of Charles Baylor McRaney
2		Office of Sheffield and Major
3		Overland Park, Kansas, December 7, YR-1, 10:00 A.M.

4

5 After having been sworn, Charles B. McRaney testified:

6

7 Examination by Mr. Sheffield:

8

9   Q: Would you state your name for the record?

10   A: Charles Baylor McRaney.

11   Q: And your profession?

12   A: I'm the Coding Supervisor at Twin Oaks Hospital here in Overland Park.

13   Q: Your age?

14   A: Fifty-five.

15   Q: Have you ever been deposed before?

16   A: No. This is my first time.

17   Q: Then you understand that the nature of this meeting is to take testimony for the court

18   proceedings initiated by my client, Ms. Grace Garrett, against your employer, Twin Oaks

19   Hospital, for violation of the federal False Claims Act. I'll ask you questions, then your own

20   attorney, Ms. Gentry, will ask you questions. I can ask you more questions after that, as

21   can she, in order. The questions and answers will be recorded by the court reporter there,

22   Ms. Lattimer. Do you understand all that?

23   A: Yes.

24   Q: You came here today in response to a subpoena, is that so? Issued by the district court?

25   A: Yes.

26   Q: And you understand that you have sworn to tell the truth here today?

27   A: Yes.

28   Q: Do you have any reservations about that oath?

29   A: No.

30   Q: Are you on any medications, stimulants, or drugs, or do you have any health problems that

31   would interfere with your testimony today?

32   A: No.

33   Q: No health problems?

34   A: Not that I know of.

35   Q: If you decide during questioning that you'd like to take a break, we'll do that, all right?

36   A: Okay.

37   Q: If you don't understand a question, you have a right to, and should ask for, clarification.

38   Is that understood?

39   A: Yes.

40   Q: If you need me to repeat a question, you just ask, and if you want to volunteer a clearer

41   answer than you gave to a previous question, just say so.

42   A: All right.

43   Q: At times, your attorney might object to a question you've been asked; if so, she'll tell you

44   whether to answer or not. The objection will be put into the record by the court reporter and

45   a judge will decide if your answer can be used at trial. Do you understand that?

46   A: Yes.

47   Q: Was there anything unclear about what I just told you?

48   A: No. I understand.

49   Q: So you can think of no reason why you cannot give full and accurate testimony here today?

50   A: No.

51   Q: All right, then, let's begin. How long have you been with Twin Oaks?

52   A: Fifteen years. Twenty years in the records area altogether.

53   Q: All right, now Mr. McRaney, your hospital admits to having treated all of the patients and

54   procedures listed in the Complaint, correct?

55   A: Yes.

56   Q: And the codes in question relate to all of these patients, yes?

57   A: Yes.

58   Q: Let's look at the physician's notes from the medical chart with regard to claim #101010-ABC,

59   which relates to one of the patients involved in this matter. I'm handing the witness a document

55

60		that I'll ask the court reporter to mark as Deposition Exhibit A. Do you recognize what's
61		written there, Mr. McRaney?
62	A:	Yes. They're the physician's notes and orders from one of our Hospital's medical charts.
63	Q:	To what do they refer?
64	A:	They refer to the progress of the patient admitted for treatment relative to pneumonia.
65	Q:	That's the same disease for which the claims in paragraphs #20 through #33 in the
66		Complaint received treatment, is it not?
67	A:	Yes.
68	Q:	The treatment lasted how long?
69	A:	Our records show that was roughly a week-long treatment.
70	Q:	The procedures on the other claims listed in the Complaint lasted the same amount of time,
71		in general?
72	A:	Yes, roughly. Some longer, some shorter, by a day.
73	Q:	All of these patients were residents of River Crest Retirement Community, true?
74	A:	Yes.
75	Q:	Now, Mr. McRaney, please read over the physician's notes with regard to claim
76		#101010-ABC.
77		
78		(MR. MCRANEY REVIEWS THE EXHIBIT.)
79		
80	Q:	I'm now handing the court reporter charts relevant to all of the other claims in this
81		Complaint, asking that they be marked, respectively and in order, Exhibits B through
82		O. Now, Mr. McRaney, would you review the exhibits being handed to you by the court
83		reporter?
84		
85		(MR. MCRANEY REVIEWS THE EXHIBITS.)
86		
87	A:	All right.
88	Q:	The physicians' notes on the left side of the charts are of the same nature as those of the
89		first?
90	A:	Yes.
91	Q:	And the orders/procedures/diagnostics on the right side of these charts are basically the
92		same as those on the first as well?
93	A:	Yes, they are.
94	Q:	And briefly—the term "stat" —means "immediately" in medical parlance, correct?
95	A:	It does.
96	Q:	And "DFW"?
97	A:	That's just an abbreviation for sugar water fluids.
98	Q:	IV means "intravenous"?
99	A:	Yes.
100	Q:	And "IM"?
101	A:	That means the medicine is administered "intra-muscularly" —the typical way, by
102		injection—rather than intravenously, "IV."
103	Q:	So if administered by IV, the situation is generally more serious than if administered IM?
104	A:	Yes. All in all.
105	Q:	And "q 4 hrs." or "q 8 hrs."?
106	A:	That means that the indicated medication should be administered within that time frame.
107	Q:	The charts in question here, they all show that the physicians in charge did not visit the
108		patients with any increased frequency during their stays, did they?
109	A:	No.
110	Q:	And some of these orders were even given by the physicians' nurses, as designated by the
111		initials R.P.N. —registered practical nurse—weren't they?
112	A:	Yes.
113	Q:	So the physicians apparently considered the patients well enough to allow that, correct?
114	A:	There are various reasons for that. I don't know why that occurred.
115	Q:	There were no consultations with pulmonary specialists ordered by the treating physicians,
116		were there?
117	A:	No.
118	Q:	These patients were all discharged from the Hospital's care? No deaths involved and no
119		transfers to a larger hospital?

120   A: No.
121   Q: Mr. McRaney, what is the difference between basic pneumonia and severe pneumococcal
122   pneumonia?
123   A: Well, the former, though serious, is the basic classification of the respiratory infection.
124   The latter is a severe respiratory infection, complicated and requiring a heightened level
125   of care.
126   Q: They have different codes under the relevant coding systems, do they not?
127   A: Of course.
128   Q: A physician treating a case of severe pneumococcal pneumonia, especially one suffered by a
129   senior citizen, would ask for a consultation with a pulmonary specialist normally?
130   A: He might.
131   Q: And he would ask for digital scans—MRIs or CTs—of the lungs?
132   A: That would be typical.
133   Q: A patient this age would be semi-comatose in this bad of a condition, with a severe
134   infection?
135   A: Perhaps. That depends on the circumstances.
136   Q: The patient would most likely be moved to intensive care if the case were that severe?
137   A: That would be common, but not in all cases.
138   Q: If a case of severe pneumococcal pneumonia was indicated, the doctor would have the lungs
139   scoped on an elevated basis, correct? So as to determine the fluid levels there?
140   A: The lungs were scoped on the patient in Exhibit A, as you can see, and at least once on a
141   majority of these patients.
142   Q: But not repeatedly?
143   A: Not repeatedly, no. But the patient in Exhibit A was still sick—elevated temperature and
144   weak upon discharge. All of the cases were the same, and all had to be taken out in a
145   wheelchair.
146   Q: Well, I was wheeled to the car when I had a broken hand. Isn't that routine at hospitals?
147   A: What's routine in most cases isn't routine in every case.
148   Q: Mr. McRaney, considering the physicians' notes regarding these claims, which reflect no
149   consultations, no heightened frequency of physicians' visits, nurses taking over visits for
150   the physicians, no digital scans, a routine lung scoping regimen, no ICU stays—in fact,
151   patients who are ambulatory—and in short nothing that reflects a severe respiratory
152   dilemma, why was each of these claims coded for severe pneumococcal pneumonia instead of
153   basic pneumonia?
154   A: Because, Mr. Sheffield, it's not that simple. You're focusing only on the physicians' notes,
155   which are notoriously cryptic and don't address everything that happened in the Hospital
156   relevant to that patient. If you look on the right side of these charts, you see that increased
157   cultures were done in these cases, and that nasal oxygen was ordered in all of them, to
158   facilitate breathing that was labored. You also see that antibiotics were increased, and
159   initially at least, nothing allowed by mouth in most cases. They were limited to semi-solid
160   foods even when they were able to eat. More X-rays were done. All of that is treatment
161   indicative of a severe condition that the physicians' notes—for whatever reason—don't
162   reflect completely. And although there's no evidence of pulmonary specialists being brought
163   in on these cases, there are notes that refer to other general practitioners being consulted.
164   As I've said, these notes are infamously obscure and don't always address or reflect things
165   that occurred or the severity of the situation. In my view, severe pneumococcal pneumonia
166   was the correct code to assign in each of these cases, not basic, uncomplicated pneumonia.
167   Q: But your confusion about this matter never became a matter of concern until the Plaintiff,
168   Ms. Garrett, brought it to your attention on June 3rd, did it?
169   A: Well, we didn't realize this was such a question until she brought it up at the meeting, no.
170   The other coders had mentioned it to me before June 3rd, and then they apparently talked
171   further with Grace about it. I don't know why. But when Grace brought it up at the staff
172   meeting, I took up the problem.
173   Q: You alone?
174   A: I did so at the direction of Rosemary Rinehart, our Hospital Administrator.
175   Q: So you called Mid-West Health Insurance, the Medicare Intermediary's office, which
176   answers questions of this nature?
177   A: Yes.
178   Q: When?
179   A: On June 10th.

180	Q:	A week after the meeting and only after Ms. Garrett asked you several times?
181	A:	I was getting to it.
182	Q:	Why so late?
183	A:	Late? That's not a long time when you're talking about a big hospital like ours, with a
184		multitude of responsibilities and billings. In fact, that's quite soon. I got to it as soon as
185		I could, especially considering that I believed—and still believe—we coded the procedure
186		correctly.
187	Q:	And with whom did you talk at the Medicare Intermediary's office, a week after you learned
188		of the problem?
189	A:	I called and talked to Lesley Ross, who works for Mid-West Health Insurance in
190		Kansas City.
191	Q:	You'd had dealings with Ms. Ross before?
192	A:	No, I'd not talked to her before. She was new.
193	Q;	So you talked to Ms. Ross on June 10th?
194	A:	No. She wasn't available at first, so I left a message and then she called me back in a few
195		days—on the 13th. Ms. Rinehart was in the office with me, and I put the call on the speaker.
196		Then I told Ms. Ross of our concern. I asked if we were correct in coding the procedures as
197		severe pneumococcal pneumonia. She noted it, and then she asked me to email her. I did
198		that on the same day, June 13th. We waited to hear, expecting a phone call. But then on
199		15th, I received a letter from her office.
200	Q:	I'm handing the witness what I ask the reporter to designate as Deposition Exhibit P.
201		Do you recognize it?
202	A:	Yes, it's a copy of the letter from Ms. Ross to me.
203	Q:	Can you read that for a moment to yourself, then when you're done, read the last paragraph
204		aloud for the record.
205		
206		(MR. MCRANEY READS THE LETTER.)
207		
208	A:	"I stress once more that this is an important matter, and that for all concerned, it should be
209		settled as soon as possible. In the meantime, if you have any other information that could
210		help prove to us that the current coding is proper, please forward it."
211	Q:	Mr. McRaney, that directive you just read states that Ms. Ross was not sure you were
212		correct, and says that she will be back in touch with you, doesn't it?
213	A:	And it also says that she thought we were doing the right thing. She said we could code as
214		we were on these claims.
215	Q:	But that's a provisional statement, isn't it Mr. McRaney? And the Intermediary said that
216		the facts appeared to warrant a finding that the code was wrong.
217	A:	It's provisional, yes, and as to her considering the code "seemingly unwarranted," she
218		admits that view is based on only a cursory reading. From our standpoint, she not only told
219		us to go forward with the higher code, she never got back in touch with us at all. All of that
220		sent a mixed message at the very least.
221	Q:	But there is no approval of your continuing to code procedures in the same way, is there?
222	A:	No. Not expressly.
223	Q:	And you proceeded to code similar procedures this way, did you not?
224	A:	We did. Of course we did.
225	Q:	Even though she said she would have to get back in touch with you about the propriety of
226		that practice?
227	A:	But she never did call back. Or write. If told to proceed until advised otherwise, and you're
228		never advised otherwise, why would you change course? That change could've been wrong
229		itself. We were obviously trying to do the right thing or we wouldn't have called at all.
230	Q:	Ms. Ross said it was an important point and needed to be figured out and answered, didn't
231		she?
232	A:	But as I said, she never contacted us about it.
233	Q:	You never called her either, did you?
234	A:	We assumed we were right. That's logical, in my opinion. If you disagree, that's yours. But
235		it's a matter of opinion only.
236	Q:	You weren't aware that Ms. Ross went on sick leave soon thereafter and hasn't returned?
237	A:	No. Of course not. How could I be? And even so, how was I or anyone to know that the
238		Intermediary's office wouldn't handle the unfinished business of one of its sick personnel?

239		It seems to me Ms. Garrett rushed to suspect us of fraud before the Intermediary's office
240		ever even responded to our inquiry.
241	Q:	Do you not have independent auditors and quality controls in place to catch mistakes in
242		coding, Mr. McRaney?
243	A:	We do, but Ms. Garrett blew the whistle before those audits—which are conducted
244		randomly—could ever be done.
245	Q:	But Mr. McRaney, you admit that you didn't call to find out why Ms. Ross had not responded
246		to what she herself termed a matter of great importance, weeks and weeks later?
247	A:	Well, the ball was in her court.
248	Q:	I see. So you left it there?
249	A:	I did.
250	Q:	This is not the first of its nature though, is it?
251	A:	What do you mean?
252	Q:	Ms. Garrett testified that your office has coded procedures such as these, in a similar
253		context, as basic pneumonia. Why are you so confused now and why did you represent to
254		Ms. Ross that you were confused?
255	A:	That's Grace's opinion. That they're the same thing. Under the circumstances we had late
256		last winter, with an epidemic of an infectious disease in a community of elderly patients,
257		living in close quarters, they're different situations in my view.
258	Q:	But you've done your kind of work for how long, Mr. McRaney?
259	A:	Twenty years.
260	Q:	And you were confused about this?
261	A:	Yes. It's not all cut and dry. If we made a mistake, we made a mistake. I don't think we
262		have, but it's just a mistake in any event. Apparently, Ms. Garrett feels she has perfect
263		knowledge about these coding decisions, but the Medicare worker herself, Ms. Ross, was
264		obviously unclear.
265	Q:	Maybe she was confused, Mr. McRaney, but were you?
266	A:	Ms. Gentry: Objection.
267	Q:	All right. Mr. McRaney, weren't there two other cases, I.D. #101000-DSK, billed April 10,
268		YR-1, and I.D. #101000-FCD, billed May 13, YR-1, that unlike the cases mentioned in the
269		Complaint, were assigned the code for basic pneumonia?
270	A:	Yes.
271	Q:	But those two cases I just mentioned were not River Crest residents, were they?
272	A:	No.
273	Q:	Why were they billed with a different code?
274	A:	For the simple reason that they were different cases from those involving the River Crest
275		residents. The patients from River Crest all had the same kind of problems. That's not
276		uncommon—people living in a retirement community often do. Especially when there's an
277		infectious disease, and it's a wintry winter, as we had last year—some of these diseases are
278		seasonal, of course.
279	Q:	And how many more files did you code this way after Ms. Ross's letter?
280	A:	After?
281	Q:	After.
282	A:	Through our inventory of the matter, a total of five after the Ross letter, involving River
283		Crest patients, but before this claim was unsealed.
284	Q:	And since you became aware of the claim?
285	A:	We haven't had a case like that since—not involving severe pneumococcal pneumonia.
286	Q:	Any involving basic pneumonia?
287	A:	Yes. Three. But none of them were River Crest patients.
288	Q:	So after the claim of fraud was brought to your attention, none involving severe
289		pneumococcal pneumonia, but three involving basic pneumonia. After the claim was
290		unsealed, none at the higher payment code, but three at the lower.
291	Ms. Gentry: Objection. That's a statement, not a question.	
292	Q:	I'll rephrase it. So you knew this was a continuing problem, the question of the correct
293		procedure, but you didn't call to find out, and persisted in the coding procedure despite
294		being forewarned of its provisional propriety?
295	A:	The cases involving that coding were continually getting paid throughout the
296		summer. That seems like more than tacit approval to me. Every one of them was paid
297		by July 31st.

298	Q:	But the confusion didn't prompt you to call?
299	A:	I have a big office and I'm in charge of a great many things. I manage a lot of business.
300		I remember telling Robert Jackson, my assistant coding supervisor, to check up on it a
301		few days after the letter. But at the time he was in transition to another job at the Hospital.
302		Then it just slipped both of our minds. At any rate, the government implied they'd get
303		back with us and to go on with what we were doing. So that's what we did. I think that
304		was reasonable. Plus, let me repeat—I believe we're coding it right. There's a difference
305		of opinion on this matter. It's not false. It's a matter of interpretation and not materially
306		different in any event.
307	Q:	The difference in payment is great though, isn't it?
308	A:	$30,000 some odd dollars a case.
309	Q:	Fifteen differences times thirty thousand dollars is $450,000 before the problem was caught.
310		That's an insubstantial amount?
311	Ms. Gentry:	Objection. That's just an assertion veiled in the form of an interrogative.
312	Mr. Sheffield:	No. Mr. McRaney stated that since this is all just a matter of interpreting some
313		language, it isn't material. But since it also involves the payment of a sum, my
314		question is aimed at determining what all went into his decision process when he
315		decided this was immaterial. So again, are you saying that $450,000 over a few
316		months time is insubstantial?
317	A:	If you put it that way, then of course it's substantial. It's a considerable sum of money. But if
318		I can answer further—which will require me to repeat myself, yet again—I believe we coded
319		it correctly, acted properly, and were owed that amount.
320	Q:	You've had security called on Ms. Garrett before, haven't you? On August 12, YR-1,
321		with regard to an incident that the Hospital Administrator later had to apologize to
322		Ms. Garrett for?
323	A:	It was a misunderstanding, one that Ms. Garrett contributed to by refusing to comply with
324		Hospital protocol, again and again.
325	Q:	But your accusations against her—for theft and trespass—were untrue, weren't they?
326	A:	I didn't know that at the time.
327	Q:	And after all of this came to light this summer, you vigorously opposed her candidature for
328		an Assistant Coding Supervisor position, didn't you Mr. McRaney?
329	A:	I certainly did. I stand by that. For reasons completely dissociated from her assertions in
330		this matter.
331	Q:	One final thing. The person hired for that position, was he or she ever apprised about this
332		controversy regarding coding procedures?
333	A:	We haven't had a chance to do that.
334	Q:	Why not?
335	A:	As I've said, things have been up in the air since the conversation with Ms. Ross.
336		I wouldn't have known yet what to tell my new assistant. Plus, we haven't had to code that
337		procedure lately.
338	Q:	No further questions. Your witness.
339		
340		Examination by Ms. Gentry:
341		
342	Q:	Mr. McRaney, was the information in dispute in this matter, namely the files that are the
343		subject of the allegations in the Complaint, open to anyone on your staff?
344	A:	Of course. The files are in our computerized records system, in our Records Office, open to
345		all our staff.
346	Q:	And in your opinion, could anyone in your office have made the objection to the coding
347		procedures that Ms. Garrett is making?
348	A:	Absolutely. The fact that the other Records Specialists saw it first, and mentioned it to her,
349		testifies to that fact.
350	Q:	But no one else who saw the codes, confused as they were at first, came to the conclusion
351		that Ms. Garrett did?
352	A:	No. They didn't.
353	Q:	Then how did all this come to your attention? How did all this get started?
354	A:	Well, when we had these cases coming in from River Crest back in the spring, I looked
355		at the medical records and made the determination that they should be coded as severe
356		pneumococcal pneumonia. The other Records Specialists apparently had some questions,
357		because they thought there was a similarity between this ailment and basic pneumonia.

358 They apparently asked Grace about it, and she brought it up at the staff meeting on
359 June 3rd, as I've said. No one else spoke up at that meeting but her. Besides, even then,
360 Grace framed her concerns in terms of a "mistake" she wondered if we were making, not in
361 terms of a "fraud" she thought we were committing.
362 Q: Were you aware of Stuart Chamberlain's press conference?
363 A: Yes, we were. At least, I was. But I certainly didn't associate what he was saying with
364 anything we were doing at Twin Oaks. We were still fumbling around for an answer at that
365 point, having contacted Ms. Ross and done our due diligence there.
366 Q: And with regard to Ms. Ross's letter. You didn't send her any proof or arguments about your
367 current practices?
368 A: No, because we weren't committed to the way we were coding as a matter of principle.
369 I mean, we think we're doing it right, but if the government thinks otherwise, then we'll
370 go with what they say. We made our case to Ms. Ross about what we were doing, but in the
371 form of a question, open to correction if she thought otherwise. We never heard otherwise,
372 so we proceeded. We didn't insert ourselves into the determination of what was basically a
373 call for Medicare to make.
374 Q: Mr. McRaney, opposing counsel asked about your professional relationship with
375 Ms. Garrett. Elaborate on that. You've objected to her observance of protocols?
376 A: Yes. Ms. Garrett has trespassed into other employees' offices, obtained passwords to their
377 computers, gotten janitorial staff to let her in places she had no right to be—that kind
378 of thing. I'd reprimanded her time and again for it. The incident on August 12th that
379 involved my calling security was because she was in my secretary's office after hours, on my
380 secretary's computer, during a time at which we'd been experiencing software theft in the
381 Hospital. As it turned out, my secretary had in fact allowed her in the office, but I couldn't
382 have known that at the time.
383 Q: She also claims that you defamed her at a company picnic?
384 A: Hardly. I was at a table consisting of the promotions committee. I had no idea Grace sent a
385 spy to record my conversation, but all I said was what I just told you, under oath, regarding
386 her presumptuousness and insubordination. I also mentioned something that relates to
387 her character—a legitimate employment interest. For months, she's been in the middle of
388 a very public, violent, and tasteless custody battle with her ex-husband. She's resented my
389 objections to her numerous requests for days off to attend court proceedings.
390 Q: In your opinion, why would Grace Garrett apply to be your assistant in the Records Office,
391 considering your working relationship was not a good one?
392 A: In my opinion, she knew that I was at the time mulling over a move myself, to take a job on
393 the West Coast. I reconsidered, however, which must've disappointed her.
394 Ms. Gentry: No further questions.
395
396 (End of Deposition: 11:30 a.m., December 7, YR-1.)
397
398 Certificate of Stenographer
399 I, Lucie Lattimer, certified stenographic reporter for the court, CSR No. 4674, do hereby certify
400 that I reported in Stenograph notes the foregoing proceedings, and that they have been edited by
401 me, or under my direction and the foregoing transcript contains a full, true, complete and accurate
402 transcript of the proceedings held in this matter, to the best of my knowledge. I further certify that
403 this transcript of the proceedings truly and correctly reflects the exhibits, if any, offered by the
404 respective parties.
405 In witness, I have subscribed my name on this 7th day of December, YR-1.
406
407
408   *Lucie K. Lattimer*
                                          Lucie K. Lattimer

EXHIBIT A

Twin Oaks Hospital

Overland Park, Kansas

Medical Record Chart # 101010-ABC

(Personal Information Redacted)

Physician's Notes	Orders/Procedures/Diagnostics
Mar. 1: 85 yr.-old male admitted this a.m.; severe cough; low grade fever; lethargic; dehydrated; lower back pain and pain upon deep inhalation; pulse moderately high— around 90; abnormal lung sounds; intermittent coughing; no known allergies; no serious medical history; bedside sputum streaky w/ blood; provisional diagnosis: upper respiratory infection; test to rule out severe respiratory infection. RSK, M.D.	Mar. 1: Nothing by mouth. Bathroom privileges with assistance. Chest x-ray, stat. Start IV: 1000 ccs of DFW q 4 hrs.; routine lab work in A.M. on Mar. 2. Start 6000 units of penicillin IM q 8 hrs. Bed rest. Repeat lab work daily. Order nasal oxygen.
Mar. 2: largely status quo but with elevated temperature; continuous cough; awaiting test results. Order lungs scoped. RSK, M.D.	Mar. 2: Medical consult w/Dr. Jerry Owens, G.P. Discontinue penicillin and elevate antibiotic to chloromycetin, one gram every six hours by IV. Continue nasal oxygen. Scope lungs for fluid level.
Mar. 3: Conditions remains the same, clinically; fever status quo; white blood count elevated; urinary output decreased; patient ambulatory in room; no noticeable pain; sits in chair; cough. RSK, M.D.	Mar. 3: Repeat chest x-ray and lab work. Start semi-solid diet.
Mar. 4: cough improved; no marked change; sputum cultures non-revealing; breathing improved; clinical improvement evident; concern about x-ray not being necessarily diagnostic of severe infection. RSK, M.D.	Mar. 4: Repeat chest x-ray and lab work. Have nurse provide assistance to walk patient twice a day.
Mar. 5: patient looks better; good appetite; improving; final culture results pending; possible discharge for Mar 6 a.m. JDI, R.P.N for RSK	Mar. 5: Solid food. Exercise with assistance as needed from staff.
Mar.6: Discharge, though with cough, elevated temp.; weak; taken to car in wheelchair. JDI, R.P.N for RSK	

[PLAINTIFF AND DEFENDANT HAVE STIPULATED THAT THE
SYMPTOMS AND TREATMENTS REFLECTED IN THE RECORDS
ACTING AS EXHIBITS "B" THROUGH "O" ARE IDENTICAL IN FORM
AND SUBSTANCE TO THOSE REFLECTED IN EXHIBIT "A"—SEE
COMPLAINT PARAGRAPH 10; ANSWER PARAGRAPH 10.]

EXHIBIT P

Mid-West Health Insurance
124 Brazelton Street
Kansas City, Missouri 64105

June 15, YR-1

Rosemary S. Rinehart
Charles B. McRaney
Office of the Administrator
Twin Oaks Hospital, Inc.
1510 Riparian Way
Overland Park, Kansas 56788

RE: Coding Inquiry in relation to basic pneumonia as opposed to severe pneumococcal pneumonia

Dear Ms. Rinehart and Mr. McRaney:

I write in answer to your telephone call of June 13, YR-1, inquiring as to the proper code assignment with regard to the above-referenced matter. At this point, I've raised your questions in my conversations with the Medicare Office. The matter is still at a preliminary stage, but since this is an important question of some consequence, I wanted to respond as soon as possible.

For the time being—and this is a provisional statement only—you can consider the code on the matters in question for severe pneumococcal pneumonia as proper, though upon a cursory reading of the facts, they seem to warrant the opposite conclusion.

I stress once more that this is an important matter, and that for all concerned, it should be settled as soon as possible. In the meantime, if you have any other information that could help prove to us that the current coding is proper, please forward it.

Thank you for contacting us.

Sincerely,

Lesley Ross

Lesley Ross
Assistant Regional Representative

1		Deposition of Rosemary Creighton Rinehart
2		Offices of Sheffield and Major
3		Overland Park, Kansas, December 7, YR-1, 2:00 P.M.
4		
5		
6		After having been sworn, Rosemary C. Rinehart testified:
7		
8		Examination by Mr. Sheffield:
9		
10	Q:	Please state your name and age for the record.
11	A:	Rosemary Creighton Rinehart. I'm fifty-nine.
12	Q:	Have you been deposed before, Ms. Rinehart?
13	A:	Yes.
14	Q:	As part of your job or for other reasons?
15	A:	Both.
16	Q:	How many times?
17	A:	Three times. Twice involving the Hospital and once involving a property dispute.
18	Q:	So you're familiar with the process?
19	A:	Yes.
20	Q:	As you may recall, this testimony is sworn, and is subject to use in the lawsuit under the
21		False Claims Act brought by Grace Garrett against her former, and your current, employer,
22		Twin Oaks Hospital.
23	A:	I understand that.
24	Q:	And you have sworn to tell the truth? No qualms about that oath?
25	A:	No qualms.
26	Q:	I'll ask questions of you, and your attorney may object to those questions and will tell you
27		whether to answer or not. But those questions will nevertheless be part of the record for a
28		judge to decide upon. Everything is being taken down by the court reporter over there. You
29		understand?
30	A:	Yes.
31	Q:	Ms. Gentry may ask you some questions later, and then I can ask you more if necessary. All
32		right?
33	A:	All right.
34	Q:	You're under no medications or suffering from any illness that would prevent your
35		unqualified testimony today, is that right?
36	A:	That's right. No medications or illnesses.
37	Q:	If you need a break we'll take one, but I think this will be a short deposition all in all.
38		There'll only be a few questions, at least from my end. If you need clarification on anything,
39		just ask me. Okay?
40	A:	Okay.
41	Q:	How long have you been the Hospital Administrator there at Twin Oaks?
42	A:	At Twin Oaks, seven years.
43	A:	And before that time?
44	Q:	I was the administrator at a county hospital in western Kansas for five years. Before
45		that, I was an assistant administrator at the same place for about fifteen. I've been in the
46		hospital administration field, in some capacity, my whole professional life.
47	Q:	For all intents and purposes, a Hospital Administrator is the chief operating officer of a
48		hospital, isn't that right? In charge of running the entire outfit?
49	A:	That's a fair assessment, yes.
50	Q:	You answer to no one but the board of directors, correct?
51	A:	Yes. That's the chain of command.
52	Q:	How big is Twin Oaks Hospital, Ms. Rinehart?
53	A:	We have 300 beds. We're going through an expansion to add another fifty.
54	Q:	And the Hospital's affiliation?
55	A:	It's a private hospital, founded in the last century, philanthropically. It has no affiliation
56		with a school or religious group.
57	Q:	When was the River Crest Retirement Community built?
58	A:	It opened in January of YR-1.
59	Q:	Its location?
60	A:	They're located about a mile down the road from us.

61	Q:	A lot of patients from there?
62	A:	Naturally, as it's close. It's a huge retirement facility with over three hundred residents
63		in various arrangements—condos, assisted living, a nursing home—all levels of
64		independence.
65	Q:	Why was there such a rash of these procedures at that time, last winter, and why did they
66		all concentrate at Twin Oaks Hospital?
67	A:	For one thing, we're the hospital that residents are sent to when they have major problems.
68		We're known for our geriatric care. For the other thing, late winter and spring is a common
69		pneumonia season, particularly among the elderly living in a community. There's nothing
70		surprising about the fact that we'd see a spike in such procedures at that time, or that we'd
71		have so many elderly patients considering that the retirement home had just opened so
72		nearby.
73	Q:	Isn't it true that you've instituted an incentive program at your hospital that rewards
74		employees for helping the Hospital establish a profit?
75	A:	We do. We encourage departments in revenue building and in expense cutting. If they're
76		justified, after a year-end audit, conducted by an independent consultant, bonuses are
77		awarded. That's good business. But as I said, we don't determine who gets those bonuses, or
78		whether the cuts or gains are worthy of remuneration. The independent auditor does that.
79		If anything is untoward, of course, we would be told and the employee reprimanded.
80	Q:	Mr. McRaney is under such an incentive program?
81	A:	All our management employees are. It was just instituted last year. Charles McRaney is one
82		of our finest, most upstanding employees. He's tough, but he's fair, and he's been recognized
83		by the Chamber of Commerce for his civic contributions and sits on the ethics advisory
84		committee there.
85	Q:	The hospital has more than a geographical closeness to River Crest though, doesn't it?
86	A:	Well, we have consultants that go there and provide blood pressure screenings and give
87		dietetic advice. We have a presence there. It's part of our community outreach. We're proud
88		of it.
89	Q;	These are nurses, though, and health care professionals who have some influence over the
90		residents there—and could advise them to seek treatment at your hospital?
91	A:	They're there to provide a service. They're a public face to our hospital, but there's no
92		pressure applied for people to come to us.
93	Q:	And who brought the subject of this claim to your attention?
94	A:	Well, first off, Ms. Garrett mentioned we might be making a mistake in the June 3rd staff
95		meeting. We always encourage our employees, especially those with such an important job
96		as coding, to let us know what kind of job we're doing and whether there are any questions
97		or confusions.
98	Q:	So Ms. Garrett was the first to bring this up, that's what you're saying?
99	A:	Yes.
100	Q:	Did Mr. McRaney have your approval of the coding procedures he was implementing, before
101		Ms. Garrett's notice to you on June 3rd and after?
102	A:	Yes. He did.
103	Q:	Have you known Mr. McRaney to be confused about coding matters, prompting the call to
104		the Medicare Intermediary?
105	A:	No. But there's always a first time, and I'd rather us call to find out the answer as we did
106		than to be belligerently wrong about something.
107	Q:	You were aware of Mr. McRaney's conflict with Ms. Garrett last August and called them into
108		conference about it?
109	A:	Yes.
110	Q:	You apologized, did you not, on behalf of the Hospital?
111	A:	I did, but I also explained to her why Mr. McRaney did so. He was following my orders to be
112		vigilant about employee protocols. We'd experienced a series of thefts around then.
113	Q:	Ms. Garrett did not get the promotion she was seeking in the Records Office, did she?
114	A:	She did not, based on factors completely separate from this incident. We found a candidate
115		that we, in our professional opinion, considered better qualified.
116	Q:	In what ways?
117	Ms. Gentry:	Objection. We agreed to a separate set of depositions regarding any claim for
118		retaliatory discharge.
119	Mr. Sheffield:	Your Witness.
120	Examination by Ms. Gentry:	

121	Q:	Has there ever been a false claims charge brought against the Hospital?
122	A:	No. None whatsoever.
123	Q:	What kind of reputation does the Hospital have?
124	A:	We've been designated one of only thirty "Hospitals of Excellence" in the country with
125		regard to all our administrative procedures—that designation provided by Quality First
126		Benchmarking, a company that reviews data on all hospitals. We were singled out for
127		commendation with regard to our commitment. A placard commemorating the award is on
128		display in my office.
129	Q:	In both Ms. Garrett's and Mr. McRaney's testimony, they speak of a confrontation that
130		occurred last August. In his report to you, what did Mr. McRaney state as the reason he
131		called security?
132	A:	Because Ms. Garrett wouldn't surrender the disc she had when asked to do so. Around that
133		time, we'd been the victims of theft in the Hospital regarding computer software. That was a
134		major concern for us, naturally. I'd instructed all of my staff to be vigilant about employees'
135		whereabouts. Mr. McRaney was following orders. In my opinion, he could not have known
136		what she was doing as she wouldn't adequately explain herself.
137	Q:	This major confrontation between them occurred exactly when?
138	A:	On August 12, YR-1.
139	Q:	That was two weeks before Ms. Garrett filed the claim against the Hospital, correct?
140	A:	Yes.
141		Ms. Gentry: Thank you. That's all. No further questions.
142		
143		(End of Deposition: 3:00 p.m., December 7, YR-1.)
144		

145   **Certificate of Stenographer**

146

147   I, Lucie Lattimer, certified stenographic reporter for the court, CSR No. 4674, do hereby certify

148   that I reported in Stenograph notes the foregoing proceedings, and that they have been edited by

149   me, or under my direction and the foregoing transcript contains a full, true, complete and accurate

150   transcript of the proceedings held in this matter, to the best of my knowledge. I further certify that

151   this transcript of the proceedings truly and correctly reflects the exhibits, if any, offered by the

152   respective parties.

153   In witness, I have subscribed my name on this 7th day of December, YR-1.

154

155

156   *Lucie K. Lattimer*

                                                  Lucie K. Lattimer

157

In The
UNITED STATES DISTRICT COURT
FOR THE DISTRICT OF KANSAS

UNITED STATES OF AMERICA <u>EX REL.</u>)
GRACE A. GARRETT,   )
)
     PLAINTIFF,   )
v.   )
)
TWIN OAKS HOSPITAL, INC.,   )
    DEFENDANT.   )
	Civ. Action No. 10-2345-DMO

DEFENDANT'S MOTION FOR SUMMARY JUDGMENT

Defendant, Twin Oaks Hospital, Inc., by its undersigned counsel, moves this Court, pursuant to Rule 56(c) of the Federal Rules of Civil Procedure, for an Order granting summary judgment in its favor on Plaintiff's Complaint. Support for this Motion is set forth in the accompanying Memorandum of Law, the attached depositions of Grace Anne Garrett, Charles Baylor McRaney, and Rosemary Creighton Rinehart, and all exhibits thereto.

Respectfully submitted,

Gail Gentry
Gail Gentry
Kansas Bar No. 0066A78
D. Kan. Bar No. 94386623
Gentry, Steyn, and Hoffman
Attorneys at Law
567 Harrison Place South
Overland Park, Kansas 64111
Telephone: 816-555-4312
Facsimile: 816-555-2111
Email: gentry@gshlaw.com
Attorney for Defendant,
Twin Oaks Hospital, Inc.

Dated: January 11, YEAR

Certificate of Service

I HEREBY CERTIFY that I caused a copy of the foregoing Motion for Summary Judgment and Memorandum of Law in Support of Defendant's Motion for Summary Judgment to be sent via U.S.P.S. Express Mail, postage prepaid, and to be delivered by hand this 11th day of January, YEAR, to counsel for the Plaintiff, William L. Sheffield, Esq., Office of Sheffield and Major, 190 Seville Place, Kansas City, Kansas 64111.

Gail Gentry
Gail Gentry
Kansas Bar No. 0066A78
D. Kan. Bar No. 94386623
Gentry, Steyn, and Hoffman
Attorneys at Law
567 Harrison Place South
Overland Park, Kansas 64111
Telephone: 816-555-4312
Facsimile: 816-555-2111
Email: gentry@gshlaw.com
Attorney for Defendant,
Twin Oaks Hospital, Inc.

In The
UNITED STATES DISTRICT COURT
FOR THE DISTRICT OF KANSAS

UNITED STATES OF AMERICA <u>EX REL.</u>)
 GRACE A. GARRETT,)
)
           PLAINTIFF,)
   v.)
)
 TWIN OAKS HOSPITAL, INC.,)
)
          DEFENDANT.)
	Civ. Action No. 10-2345-DMO

PLAINTIFF'S RESPONSE TO DEFENDANT'S MOTION FOR SUMMARY JUDGMENT

Plaintiff/Relator Grace A. Garrett, by her undersigned counsel, hereby responds to Defendant's Motion for Summary Judgment, and requests that this Honorable Court deny Defendant's Motion with Prejudice, and in support thereof provides the attached Memorandum of Law in Opposition to Defendant's Motion for Summary Judgment and the attached depositions of Grace Anne Garrett, Charles Baylor McRaney, and Rosemary Creighton Rinehart, and all exhibits thereto.

Respectfully submitted,

William L.Sheffield
William L. Sheffield
Kansas Bar No. 9203B90
D. Kan. Bar No. 0020220
Office of Sheffield and Major
190 Seville Place
Kansas City, Kansas 64111
Telephone: 816-900-4220
Facsimile: 816-900-4221
Email:
shef@sheffieldand major.com
Attorney for Plaintiff/Relator,
Grace A. Garrett

Dated: January 12, YEAR

Certificate of Service

I HEREBY CERTIFY that I caused a copy of the foregoing Plaintiff's Response to Defendant's Motion for Summary Judgment and Memorandum of Law in Opposition to Defendant's Motion for Summary Judgment to be sent via U.S.P.S. Express Mail, postage prepaid, and to be delivered by hand this 12th day of January YEAR, to counsel for Defendant, Gail Gentry, Esq., Gentry, Steyn, and Hoffman, 567 Harrison Place, Overland Park, Kansas 64111.

William L.Sheffield
William L. Sheffield
Kansas Bar No. 9203B90
D. Kan. Bar No. 0020220
Office of Sheffield and Major
190 Seville Place
Kansas City, Kansas 64111
Telephone: 816-900-4220
Facsimile: 816-900-4221
Email:
shef@sheffieldandmajor.com
Attorney for Plaintiff/Relator,
Grace A. Garrett

Assignment 8

ORAL DEFENSE OF FCA MOTION'S BRIEF

Sheffield and Major
190 Seville Place
Kansas City, Kansas 64111
Telephone: 816-900-4220
Facsimile: 816-900-4221
Email: shef@sheffieldandmajor.com

INTEROFFICE MEMORANDUM

From: William Sheffield
To: Associate
Date: Today, YEAR
Re: Grace Garrett v. Twin Oaks Hospital, Inc.

Prepare an oral argument of the motion's brief written with regard to the above-referenced matter. The argument will be held in the federal District Court of Kansas. The judge will allot the time limits and the argument protocols set out in the attachment to this letter.

Gentry, Steyn, and Hoffman
Attorneys at Law
567 Harrison Place South
Overland Park, Kansas 64111
Telephone: 816-555-4312
Facsimile: 816-555-2111
Email: gentry@gshlaw.com

INTEROFFICE MEMORANDUM

From: Gale Gentry
To: Associate
Re: Grace Garrett v. Twin Oaks Hospital, Inc.
Date: Today, YEAR.

Prepare an oral argument of the motion's brief written with regard to the above-referenced matter. The argument will be held in the federal District Court of Kansas. The judge will allot the time limits and the argument protocols set out in the attachment to this letter.

Assignment 9

APPELLATE BRIEF: FCA

Sheffield and Major
190 Seville Place
Kansas City, Kansas 64111
Telephone: 816-900-4220
Facsimile: 816-900-4221
Email: shef@sheffieldandmajor.com

INTEROFFICE MEMORANDUM

From: William Sheffield
To: Associate
Date: Today, YEAR
Re: Grace Garrett v. Twin Oaks Hospital, Inc.

As you know, Judge Oher has handed down his order with regard to the above-referenced matter. An appeal has been requested and granted. The order and all appellate documents are attached. Review these materials and draft an appellate brief to the Tenth Circuit.

Gentry, Steyn, and Hoffman
Attorneys at Law
567 Harrison Place South
Overland Park, Kansas 64111
Telephone: 816-555-4312
Facsimile: 816-555-2111
Email: gentry@gshlaw.com

INTEROFFICE MEMORANDUM

From: Gale Gentry
To: Associate
Re: Grace Garrett v. Twin Oaks Hospital, Inc.
Date: Today, YEAR.

As you know, Judge Oher has handed down his order with regard to the above-referenced matter. An appeal has been requested and granted. The order and all appellate documents are attached. Review these materials and draft an appellate brief to the Tenth Circuit.

Assignment 10

MEDIATION: FCA

**THE UNITED STATES COURT OF APPEALS FOR THE TENTH
CIRCUIT
The Byron White U.S. Courthouse
1823 Stout Street, Denver, CO 80257
1-303-555-0987**

Today, YEAR

Via Electronic and U.S. Mail

Gale Gentry, Esq.
Gentry, Steyn, and Hoffman
Attorneys at Law
567 Harrison Place South
Overland Park, Kansas 64111

William L. Sheffield
Sheffield and Major
190 Seville Place
Kansas City, Kansas 64111

Re: <u>Garrett v. Twin Oaks Hospital, Inc.</u>, No. 10-1180

Dear Counsel:

The Circuit Mediation Office of the United States Court of Appeals for the Tenth Circuit has selected this appeal for inclusion in the court's Mediation Program. The mediator assigned to your case is:

Lane Bradley, Esq.
lbb@cmooffice.net

A copy of the mediator's biography is enclosed. If you have any concerns about the impartiality of the assigned mediator, including any bias that might be perceived by others, please email the Circuit Mediation Office at the address listed above immediately. Describe any and all past relationships the assigned mediator has had with counsel, counsel's firm or the parties, and any conflicts you believe the assigned mediator might have.

Assuming no conflict exists, please contact the above-referenced mediator within five days of the date of this letter to discuss the logistics of the conference. To familiarize yourself with the general guidelines of the conference process, you are asked to review the information located at the Mediation Office's website: http://www.ca10.uscourts.gov/cmo/faq.php

The website explains the confidentiality responsibilities of the mediator. Each party, party representative, attorney and person, party or attorney assisting them also must maintain confidentiality with respect to any settlement communications made or received during or incident to the mediation process.

Each party is to be represented at the mediation by its principal attorney and by a party representative with actual settlement authority.

Do not hesitate to contact me directly at 303-555-0987 if I may be of further assistance. I wish you success in your conference.

Sincerely,

Celeste Miller

Celeste Miller
Assistant Appellate Conference
Attorney

CDM/bdd

cc: Lane Bradley, Esq.

Lane Bradley, Esq.
Circuit Mediation Office
United States Court of Appeals for the Tenth Circuit
The Byron White U.S. Courthouse
1823 Stout Street, Denver, CO 80257
lbb@cmooffice.net

Today, YEAR

Gale Gentry, Esq.
Gentry, Steyn, and Hoffman
Attorneys at Law
567 Harrison Place South
Overland Park, Kansas 64111

William L. Sheffield
Sheffield and Major
190 Seville Place
Kansas City, Kansas 64111

Re: <u>Garret v. Twin Oaks Hospital, Inc.</u>., No. 10-1180

Dear Counsel:

The Circuit Mediation Office of the U.S. Court of Appeals for the Tenth Circuit previously contacted you to let you know that your case is included in the Court's Mediation Program. I will be the mediator for your case, and I look forward to working with you. If at any time during this process you have questions or concerns about the mediation, please let me know and I will be glad to help. Of course, if we fail to settle your case during this scheduled conference, I am available to continue working with you if follow-up discussions or conference sessions seem useful.

This letter serves to confirm the date, time and location for the initial scheduled conference, to give you further details about the conference itself, and to explain what you need to do in preparation.

Date: Month, Day, YEAR, starting at 9:30 A.M.
Location: TBA

For some of you, this may be the first time you have participated in any settlement conference, while others of you may be familiar with such programs but less familiar with the Tenth Circuit's version of the process. Therefore, please review the information on our website sent to you by the Mediation Office: http://www.ca10.uscourts.gov/cmo/faq.php

The most important aspects of mediation that distinguish it from litigation are the parties' control over the resolution of their dispute and its confidentiality. The conference allows the parties to explore options for resolving their dispute that include but also extend beyond the legal options available in court. Procedurally, the conference program is a flexible process, consisting of a mix of joint sessions and individual caucuses in which parties can discuss the legal and non-legal issues in their dispute, candidly weigh the strengths and weaknesses of their positions, and consider possible legal and non-legal solutions. Throughout this process, confidentiality protects any information related to the case. The fact that a case is in conference is not disclosed to the Court or to the public, and the outcome of the conference is likewise confidential unless all parties agree otherwise. In addition, information that you may disclose during your individual caucuses will not be shared with the other side, except to the extent that you authorize.

Prior to our mediation, I need you to send me the following two documents:

1. A list with the full names of anyone attending the conference on your client's behalf.
2. A Confidential Conference Statement ("CCS") that responds to the issues outlined below. The CCS can be sent by paper to my address above, or via email [lbb@cmooffice.net] or fax (303-555-0988). **Do not send your CCS to the Clerk's Office.** The content of your CCS is confidential and will not be shared with any other party or with the Court.

Other than the conference itself, your preparation of the CCS is the most important element in the conference process. Preparing your CCS allows you, your client, and me, to have a candid view of the factual and legal hurdles that you face, the strengths and weaknesses of both sides' cases, and possible avenues to settlement. Although there is no page limit to a CSS, it is generally 2-4 pages long, depending on the complexity of the issues; it is deliberately intended to be brief but candid and thorough. The Tenth Circuit and its mediators have found that the most useful CCSs follow these guidelines:

A. Please give a brief <u>factual background</u> of the case, indicating any facts that are genuinely in dispute, and why.
B. Identify <u>any cases involving the same parties</u> that are either pending or decided in any tribunal.
C. Identify any controlling or particularly relevant <u>legal authorities</u>. If these authorities are not readily available, please enclose a copy or a link where they can be reviewed.
D. Identify any <u>jurisdictional issues</u> that have been raised by any party, and give your honest assessment of the merits of these claims.
E. Is there any <u>additional information</u> that you need (from the other side, or elsewhere) before agreeing to settle? If so, how might that information be obtained?

F. Give an honest discussion of <u>your claims and defenses</u>. Please identify the strongest and weakest parts of your case and explain—legally or otherwise—their strengths and weaknesses.

G. Give an honest discussion of <u>the strongest and weakest aspects of the other side's case</u>.

H. What, in your candid assessment, is the <u>likely outcome</u> if this case continues to the Fifth Circuit on appeal?

I. Give a brief history of any <u>prior settlement negotiations,</u> and include your candid assessment as to why the case has not settled.

J. Explain any elements that your client <u>cannot compromise</u>. Identify any interests or issues that are not directly involved in this case but that might frustrate or assist in settlement.

K. A list of <u>possible settlement terms and ideas</u>. Alongside each idea, please evaluate candidly the merits of that idea and how it might be achieved.

As you prepare for conference, do not hesitate to contact me if I can be of any assistance. I wish you success in your conference endeavor.

Sincerely,

Lane Bradley
Lane Bradley, Esq.

cc: Celeste Miller

Assignment 11
_____
SETTLEMENT: FCA

Sheffield and Major
190 Seville Place
Kansas City, Kansas 64111
Telephone: 816-900-4220
Facsimile: 816-900-4221
Email: shef@sheffieldandmajor.com

INTEROFFICE MEMORANDUM

From: William Sheffield
To: Associate
Date: Today, YEAR
Re: Grace Garrett v. Twin Oaks Hospital, Inc.

As you know, we have reached an agreement with Twin Oaks Hospital, Inc. to settle Ms. Garrett's suit against the hospital. The basic terms of the agreement are reflected in the attachment to this letter.

Please draft a settlement agreement reflecting these terms, and make sure that Ms. Garrett's interests are protected accordingly. Of course, the attorney with the Department of Justice, opposing counsel, and the Court will want to review this document before any of the parties sign.

WLL:bb

Gentry, Steyn, and Hoffman
Attorneys at Law
567 Harrison Place South
Overland Park, Kansas 64111
Telephone: 816-555-4312
Facsimile: 816-555-2111
Email: gentry@gshlaw.com

INTEROFFICE MEMORANDUM

From: Gale Gentry
To: Associate
Re: Grace Garrett v. Twin Oaks Hospital, Inc.
Date: Today, YEAR.

As you know, we have reached an agreement with Grace Garrett to settle her suit against the hospital. The basic terms of the agreement are reflected in the attachment to this letter.

Please draft a settlement agreement reflecting these terms, and make sure that Twin Oaks Hospital is protected from any and all future claims with regard to this matter. Pay particular attention to secure compliance with any federal requirements. Of course, opposing counsel and the Court will want to review this document before Ms. Garrett signs.

GG: mc

Assignment 12

TRIAL PRACTICE: FCA

Sheffield and Major
190 Seville Place
Kansas City, Kansas 64111
Telephone: 816-900-4220
Facsimile: 816-900-4221
Email: shef@sheffieldandmajor.com

INTEROFFICE MEMORANDUM

From: William Sheffield
To: Associate
Date: Today, YEAR
Re: Grace Garrett v. Twin Oaks Hospital, Inc.

Prepare for trial in the above-referenced matter, Grace Garrett's FCA claim. Any of the named witnesses may be called to prove the case. No other witness or information other than that set out below (and exhibits thereto) will be allowed by the court.

1.   Deposition of Charles McRaney
2.   Deposition of Grace Garrett
3.   Deposition of Rosemary Rinehart

The case is being heard in federal court, in the federal District Court of Kansas. Notification of witnesses and general court rules as to deadlines and other matters, already provided, should be observed at all times.

Gentry, Steyn, and Hoffman
Attorneys at Law
567 Harrison Place South
Overland Park, Kansas 64111
Telephone: 816-555-4312
Facsimile: 816-555-2111
Email: gentry@gshlaw.com

INTEROFFICE MEMORANDUM

From: Gale Gentry
To: Associate
Re: Grace Garrett v. Twin Oaks Hospital, Inc.
Date: Today, YEAR.

Prepare for trial in the above-referenced matter, Twin Oaks Hospital's defense against Grace Garrett's FCA action. Any of the named witnesses may be called to rebut Ms. Garrett's claim. No other witness or information other than that set out below (and exhibits thereto) will be allowed by the court.

1.   Deposition of Charles McRaney
2.   Deposition of Grace Garrett
3.   Deposition of Rosemary Rinehart

The case is being heard in federal court, in the federal District Court of Kansas. Notification of witnesses and general court rules as to deadlines and other matters, already provided, should be observed at all times.

Assignment 13
_____

PLEADINGS: AKS

Leland, Hayes, and Leland
4566 Ashleigh Court Plaza
Kansas City, Kansas 64343
Telephone: 816-900-1029
Facsimile: 816-900-8364

MEMORANDUM

From: Candace Hayes
To: Associate
Date: Today, YR-1
Re: David E. Barrier, M.D., FCA Claim

David E. Barrier, a forty-one-year-old orthopedic surgeon here in Overland Park, Kansas, came to our office about an employment matter he believes involves a Medicare kickback scheme between Twin Oaks Hospital (the "Hospital") and a multi-specialty doctors' partnership, The Crenshaw Group, LLP ("CG").

Dr. Barrier has a five-member partnership of his own that focuses on orthopedic surgery. He is on the staff of several hospitals in the area, including Twin Oaks.

CG has thirty-five members overseen by Dr. Andrew Crenshaw, M.D., the managing partner. CG's website states that a major focus of its practice involves geriatrics, i.e., medical specialties centering on the needs of senior citizens. In addition to its practice, CG owns three retirement communities in the area: River Crest; Bluff View; and Valley Terrace. All have a variety of living arrangements, from independent living to total nursing care. River Crest, which is located near the Hospital and which opened in January, YR-1, also has a Pavilion Complex on its campus. The complex is a large indoor facility that has proved a popular venue for civic events of all types.

According to Dr. Barrier, the Hospital entered into a five-year service contract with CG, dated February 28, YR-1, under which CG would oversee a series of six health fairs per year, open to the public, in January, March, May, July, September, and November. The contract is for five years. The fee payable to CG is $25,000 for the entire contract term. Each of the retirement communities owned by CG would host one of the fairs every year, with the remaining three to be conducted at a civic center downtown.

This year, despite the terms of the contract, only two of the fairs have taken place, and both were held at the River Crest Pavilion Complex. The Hospital paid all expenses, including food, entertainment, and transportation for senior citizens, and it staffed the fairs with its own personnel. The Hospital advertised the fairs in newspapers and on websites targeted at senior citizens. The events, which were well attended, had an entrance fee that was discounted for senior citizens. No other physician or medical group participated in these fairs.

Prior to the service contract with CG, the fairs had been overseen by in-house staff at the Hospital and were conducted on the Hospital grounds. While there are six fairs per year under the present CG contract, there were only three under the old arrangement. Dr. Barrier has learned from Julia B. Courtland, the former Hospital employee in charge of the events before the CG contract, that the budget for the fairs was doubled after CG took charge of their oversight. Before she left the Hospital, Ms. Courtland expressed her concern to Rosemary C. Rinehart, the Hospital administrator, as to the propriety of the arrangement with such a large source of Medicare referrals. However, no further action was taken by the Hospital as far as Ms. Courtland knew. Ms. Courtland has also complained that Dr. Crenshaw was given a voice in the staffing at the Hospital, as he was personally responsible for her not receiving a post for which she had applied.

Dr. Barrier states that a major portion of CG's overall Medicare referrals goes to Twin Oaks each year, and that a major portion of those referrals comes from CG's three retirement communities. The fairs, in his opinion, generate new customers for CG, which in turn provide a pool of Medicare referrals for the Hospital.

At this point, we intend to pursue a claim against both the Hospital and The Crenshaw Group under the federal False Claims Act 31 U.S.C. § 3729(a) (1)(A)-(B) (2006) ("FCA") by way of the federal Anti-Kickback statute, 42 U.S.C. § 1320a-7b(b) (2006). According to the Affordable Care Act of 2010 (the "ACA"), a violation of the federal Anti-Kickback statute, 42 U.S.C. § 1320a-7b(b) (2006), will be considered a false claim under the False Claims Act. *Id* § 1320a-7b(g). Further, the ACA amends the Anti-Kickback statute so that a showing of specific intent is no longer required to establish a violation of the section. *See* Patient Protection and Affordable Health Care Act 42, U.S.C. § 1320a-7b(h).

Look into this matter, using the attached case, *United States ex rel. Conner v. Salina Regional Health Center, Inc.*, 543 F.3d 1211 (10th Cir. 2008), to acquaint yourself with the facts necessary to file a valid complaint under the FCA when a kickback is the underlying claim.

One other thing to note: The Hospital was the subject of a separate, unrelated whistleblower suit two years ago brought by another party involving leased equipment. The claim was settled by agreement between the Hospital and the Department of Health and Human Services ("HHS") dated March 15, YR-2. As part of that settlement agreement, the Hospital agreed for a term of three years from date that each and every claim made by the Hospital for reimbursement from HHS was conditional upon an express certification that the Hospital had not violated the FCA or the AKS.

Draft the complaint with the following addresses:

David E. Barrier: 127 Grant Avenue, Overland Park, Kansas, 56711

Twin Oaks Hospital, Inc.: 1510 Riparian Way, Overland Park, Kansas 56788

CG: Overland Park Medical Plaza, 3500 Riparian Way, Overland Park, Kansas 56788

Warnock and Bailey
Attorneys at Law
187 Las Cruces Boulevard
Overland Park, Kansas 56788
Telephone: 316-555-6398
Facsimile: 316-555-9852
Email: chadw@wandb.com

MEMORANDUM

From: Chad Warnock
To: Associate
Date: Today, YR-1
Re: Twin Oaks Hospital matter

Rosemary Rinehart, the Hospital Administrator at Twin Oaks Hospital, our client, has come to this firm about a lawsuit that has been filed against the hospital. According to the complaint, the following facts are alleged:

David E. Barrier, a forty-one-year-old orthopedic surgeon here in Overland Park, Kansas, has alleged a Medicare kickback scheme between Twin Oaks Hospital (the "Hospital") and a multi-specialty doctors' partnership, The Crenshaw Group, LLP ("CG").

Dr. Barrier has a five-member partnership of his own that focuses on orthopedic surgery. He is on the staff of several hospitals in the area, including Twin Oaks.

CG has thirty-five members overseen by Dr. Andrew Crenshaw, M.D., the managing partner. CG's website states that a major focus of its practice involves geriatrics, i.e., medical specialties centering on the needs of senior citizens. In addition to its practice, CG owns three retirement communities in the area: River Crest; Bluff View; and Valley Terrace. All have a variety of living arrangements, from independent living to total nursing care. River Crest, which is located near the Hospital and which opened in January, YR-1, also has a Pavilion Complex on its campus. The complex is a large indoor facility that has proved a popular venue for civic events of all types.

According to Dr. Barrier, the Hospital entered into a five-year service contract dated February 28, YR-1 with CG under which CG would oversee a series of six health fairs per year, open to the public, in January, March, May, July, September, and November. The contract is for five years. The fee payable to CG is $25,000 for the entire contract term. Each of the retirement communities owned by CG would host one of the fairs every year, with the remaining three to be conducted at a civic center downtown.

This year, despite the terms of the contract, only two of the fairs have taken place and both were held at the River Crest Pavilion Complex. The Hospital paid all expenses, including food, entertainment, and transportation for senior citizens, and it staffed the fairs with its own personnel. The Hospital advertised the fairs in newspapers and on websites targeted at senior citizens, and the events, which were well attended, had an entrance fee that was discounted for senior citizens. No other physician or medical group participated in these fairs.

Prior to the service contract with CG, the fairs had been overseen by in-house staff at the Hospital and were conducted on the Hospital grounds. While there are six fairs per year under the present CG contract, there were only three under the old arrangement. Dr. Barrier has learned from Julia B. Courtland, the former Hospital employee in charge of the events before the CG contract, that the budget for the fairs was doubled after CG took charge of their oversight. Before she left the Hospital, Ms. Courtland expressed her concern to Rosemary C. Rinehart, the Hospital administrator, as to the propriety of the arrangement with such a large source of Medicare referrals. However, no further action was taken by the Hospital as far as Ms. Courtland knew. Ms. Courtland has also complained that Dr. Crenshaw was given a voice in the staffing at the Hospital, and was personally responsible for her removal from any involvement with the fairs.

Dr. Barrier alleges that a major portion of CG's overall Medicare referrals goes to Twin Oaks each year, and that a major portion of those referrals comes from CG's three retirement communities. The fairs, in his opinion, generate new customers for CG, which in turn provide a pool of Medicare referrals for the Hospital.

Dr. Barrier is pursuing a claim against Twin Oaks under the federal False Claims Act 31 U.S.C. § 3729(a)(1)(A)-(B) (2006) ("FCA") by way of the federal Anti-Kickback statute, 42 U.S.C. § 1320a-7b(b) (2006). While CG was originally a co-defendant in this suit, it was dismissed from the action by court order dated November 6, YR-1.

The complaint is attached. Draft an answer to the complaint.

Assignment 14

BRIEF: AKS CLAIM

Leland, Hayes, and Leland
4566 Ashleigh Court Plaza
Kansas City, Kansas 64343
Telephone: 816-900-1029
Facsimile: 816-900-8364

MEMORANDUM

From: Candace Hayes
To: Associate
Date: Today, YR-1
Re: Barrier v. Twin Oaks Hospital, Inc.

As you are aware, Twin Oaks Hospital has filed a Motion for Summary Judgment in the above-referenced matter. Dr. Barrier intends to file a Response to that Motion. Please draft a memorandum of law in opposition to the Motion for Summary Judgment.

Warnock and Bailey
Attorneys at Law
187 Las Cruces Boulevard
Overland Park, Kansas 56788
Telephone: 316-555-6398
Facsimile: 316-555-9852
Email: chadw@wandb.com

MEMORANDUM

From: Chad Warnock
To: Associate
Date: Today, YR-1
Re: Barrier v. Twin Oaks Hospital, Inc.

As you are aware, Twin Oaks Hospital has filed a Motion for Summary Judgment in the above-referenced matter. Please draft a memorandum of law in support of the Motion for Summary Judgment.

Deposition of David E. Barrier, M.D.

Office of Warnock and Bailey

Kansas City, Kansas, December 1, YR-1, 10:00 A.M.

After having been sworn, David E. Barrier testified:

Examination by Mr. Warnock:

Q: For the record, state your full name and age.

A: David Emory Barrier. I'm forty-one years old.

Q: Your address?

A: 127 Grant Avenue, Overland Park, Kansas.

Q: Have you ever been deposed before, Dr. Barrier?

A: No, I haven't.

Q: All right. For clarity's sake, a deposition, which you're about to give, is sworn testimony that can be used in the court proceeding you've instituted under the False Claims Act against your former employer, Twin Oaks Hospital. I'll ask you questions, then your own attorney may do the same, and so forth. The court reporter will record all this. Do you understand?

A: Yes.

Q: You came here today in response to a subpoena from the federal district court here in Kansas City, correct?

A: Yes.

Q: And you've sworn to tell the truth today?

A: Yes.

Q: Do you have any qualifications about that oath?

A: No.

Q: Are you on any medication, stimulants, or drugs, or do you have any health problems that would interfere with your testimony?

A: No.

Q: We can take a break any time you'd like. You just say so. All right?

A: Yes.

Q: If you don't understand a question, I'll rephrase it for you. Or if you didn't hear it, I'll be glad to repeat it. Just ask.

A: Okay.

Q: Now, your attorney has the right to object to something I ask, and she'll tell you whether to proceed with a response. The objection, at any rate, will go into the record for the court to decide whether the substance of the statement is admissible at trial. Okay?

A: Yes.

Q: Was there anything unclear about what I just told you?

A: No. I understand.

Q: So you can think of no reason why you cannot give full and accurate testimony here today?

A: No.

Q: All right then. Dr. Barrier, you're a physician in Overland Park, Kansas, correct?

A. Yes.

Q: What kind of physician?

A: I'm an orthopedic surgeon.

Q: Which means you do surgical work related to bones and joints. Is that right?

A: Basically, yes.

Q: Where did you train, Dr. Barrier?

A: I went to medical school at Kansas, then did my residency at Campbell Clinic in Memphis, Tennessee.

Q: And you practice in a partnership?

A: Yes, I'm one of five surgeons, all orthopedic, in Overland Park Bone and Joint Clinic here in town.

Q: When did you form that partnership?

A: About five years ago.

Q: You were part of another partnership before that though, correct?

60	A:	For two years, right after completing my residency, I was associated with The Crenshaw
61		Group.
62	Q:	Which was formerly a defendant in this suit, correct?
63	A:	Yes.
64	Q:	And why did you leave the group?
65	A:	I wanted to strike out on my own. They intended to form a multi-specialty group—taking
66		in specialists in several areas, to create a kind of "multi-purpose" conglomerate that could
67		serve a patient's many needs. They of course eventually did go that way, but I wanted to
68		continue to concentrate on orthopedic surgery. That was the original idea—Dr. Crenshaw's
69		group had that exclusive focus at its inception—so we didn't see eye to eye on the future of
70		the association. As a result, I left to form my own group.
71	Q:	You recruited your partners?
72	A:	Yes, I'm the managing partner.
73	Q:	And you have privileges at Twin Oaks Hospital, Dr. Barrier? You're admitted to their
74		staff?
75	A:	Yes. I was brought onto the staff seven years ago.
76	Q:	Do you have privileges at other hospitals in the area?
77	A:	Yes. At St. Michael's and at Overland Park Regional.
78	Q:	Is it fair to say that you're in competition with The Crenshaw Group for patients?
79	A:	Well, to the degree we overlap, yes.
80	Q:	Now, Dr. Barrier, your medical practice is conducted from a building that you own, isn't
81		that right?
82	A:	Yes.
83	Q:	It's located near the defendant hospital, only a few blocks away?
84	A:	A few blocks.
85	Q:	All right, now Dr. Barrier, you're of course aware of the health fairs that Twin Oaks
86		conducts, as they're the subject of this lawsuit?
87	A:	Yes.
88	Q:	You object to the propriety of the relationship between my client, Twin Oaks Hospital, and
89		The Crenshaw Group with regards to a service contract, dated February 28, YR-1, in which
90		the group is commissioned to oversee six of those fairs per year. That's so?
91	A:	Yes.
92	Q:	You object to the amount the doctors are being paid, claiming that it's disproportionately
93		large for what they're asked to do in the oversight of these events?
94	A:	Well, all they do—the doctors, that is—is speak at seminars. They don't work too hard, it
95		doesn't seem to me, but the price they're paid is not my main objection.
96	Q:	Then you object to the fact that they're qualified to conduct these health fairs?
97	A:	Of course not. They're imminently qualified physicians. I've never said anything to the
98		contrary.
99	Q;	Then you must object to the quality of the health fairs? Those attending are not given
100		what they're promised, or the doctors are not performing what they've said they
101		would do?
102	A:	I've heard nothing of the kind, and those aren't the grounds of my suit.
103	Q:	Then what exactly is your objection to this contract, Dr. Barrier?
104	A:	I object to the fact that the hospital spends a great deal of money for six health fairs—
105		only two of which were performed last year—at a facility owned by The Crenshaw Group,
106		intended to bring in Medicare-related business for The Crenshaw Group, which will then be
107		referred to Twin Oaks Hospital.
108	Q:	But the health fairs aren't to be conducted only at River Crest, are they? You know of the
109		circumstances that required one of the fairs to be moved to River Crest from another site,
110		and that the other was postponed due to a facility problem at the downtown civic center?
111	A:	I know that's what they say.
112	Q:	So that I understand you, Dr. Barrier, you're of the opinion that a business arrangement
113		between the hospital and one of your major competitors that's meant to attract potential
114		patients should be considered a violation of federal law, is that right?
115	Ms. Hayes:	Objection. You're characterizing the witness's response.
116	Q:	I'll move on. This concern you have with the service contract between the hospital and The
117		Crenshaw Group—did you voice your objection to Ms. Rinehart about it?
118	A:	On numerous occasions.
119	Q:	Never in writing, though?

120	A:	No, but I told her again and again that I thought it was unfair, all the money and time
121		and trouble they were putting into these fairs. I said that they were nothing more than
122		advertising billboards for Twin Oaks and the guys at The Crenshaw Group.
123	Q:	And she responded with an offer, didn't she?
124	A:	I wouldn't call it that.
125	Mr. Warnock:	I'd like to submit to the court reporter a copy of a letter, written on Twin Oaks
126		Hospital stationery, signed by Rosemary Rinehart as Hospital Administrator,
127		dated June 4, YR-1, and have it marked Deposition Exhibit A.
128		
129	(The exhibit is marked)	
130		
131	Mr. Warnock:	I'm now handing the exhibit to the witness. Dr. Barrier, you recognize this letter?
132		
133	A:	Yes, it's a copy of the original that I received last year.
134	Q:	It's addressed to you, is it not?
135	A:	Yes.
136	Q:	Would you read aloud for the court the second paragraph?
137	A:	"Would you join us on each of the dates, at a prorated share of the fee to be paid? We'd of
138		course love to have you as part of the events. They are all-day affairs, as you know, and on
139		Saturdays. Let me know if we can work something out."
140	Q:	You refused that offer, didn't you, Dr. Barrier?
141	A:	Yes.
142	Q:	So you complained of the arrangement between your competitor and the hospital, accusing
143		Twin Oaks of playing favorites and characterizing the whole affair as an advertisement, but
144		you refused a similar offer?
145	A:	I did. I believe the whole motivation for the thing is unseemly and meant as a quid pro quo
146		for Medicare referrals.
147	Q:	But didn't you state to Ms. Rinehart in answer to this letter that you weren't willing to
148		devote six Saturdays a year at such a price?
149	A:	I had to have something to say. I didn't want to make a flat out accusation of what
150		I suspected.
151	Q:	But you never brought it up again, did you? You never responded when she told you that
152		the fee was only a nominal amount, as the intention was to develop goodwill, not to gain a
153		profit. You never said another word about it until you filed this lawsuit, did you?
154	A:	I didn't bring it up again until I'd learned more.
155	Q:	And what more you learned, you learned from Julia Courtland, did you not?
156	A:	Yes. She contacted me.
157	Q:	After she left the hospital's employ, correct?
158	A:	I'm not sure about the date. It was sometime last July. Maybe it was after she left the
159		hospital, but nevertheless, she told me about the fact The Crenshaw Group wasn't paying a
160		dime for these fairs, but they were getting all the benefit.
161	Q:	How did she contact you?
162	A:	By phone.
163	Q:	Why would she contact you?
164	A:	We grew up together in the same neighborhood here in Overland Park. Our families are
165		friends. She's been proud of my success here and I've been proud of hers. I was sorry to
166		hear she'd left the hospital, and was surprised with the news about the deal The Crenshaw
167		Group was getting on the fairs.
168	Q:	Just to confirm, Dr. Barrier, you're a member of a five-member firm, correct?
169	A:	That's what I said earlier.
170	Q:	Are you familiar with the needs of a large practice like The Crenshaw Group?
171	A:	I was an associate partner there for two years, so I'm familiar with their practice.
172	Q:	But the firm was not thirty-five members at that time, was it?
173	A:	No.
174	Q:	How big was it then?
175	A:	Ten doctors.
176	Q:	So it has more than tripled in size since you were there?
177	A:	I suppose.
178	Q:	And it had a sole focus at the time, did it not? Orthopedic work was all that they did then?
179	A:	Yes.

180	Q:	And you had no part of managing the practice at that time?
181	A:	No.
182	Q:	Have you ever managed any practice other than your own at present?
183	A:	No, I haven't.
184	Q:	So you're not an expert on the kinds of "deals," as you call them, such a large practice might
185		receive, are you?
186	A:	I know a free deal when I see one. You don't have to be an expert to recognize that.
187	Q:	Dr. Barrier, after Ms. Courtland called you, did you ask Ms. Rinehart about the service
188		contract between the hospital and The Crenshaw Group directly?
189	A:	Not directly. I bumped into her at the hospital last spring and remember asking about a
190		sweet deal that they were giving Crenshaw. She just shrugged and walked off. She was very
191		cool to me.
192	Q:	By "cool" you mean she didn't want to discuss another party's contract with you?
193	A:	I didn't ask her about another party's contract. Not specifically, as I just said.
194	Q:	Tell me, Dr. Barrier, do you refer patients to all the hospital at which you have
195		privileges?
196	A:	Of course.
197	Q:	Some more than others?
198	A:	It would depend. Various things contribute to where a patient is referred.
199	Q:	So some years, more of your patients might be referred to one than another?
200	A:	Yes, as I said, it's relative.
201	Q:	Haven't hospitals appealed to you, hoping for your business and trying to accommodate your
202		practice?
203	A:	Yes.
204	Q:	But when you send them business, that's not a kickback, is it?
205	A:	It's not. Not everything is a quid pro quo. But some things definitely are.
206	Q:	But when we're talking about referral patterns, appearances don't explain everything, do
207		they Dr. Barrier, as you've just admitted?
208	A:	Not everything. But they do explain some things.
209	Q:	Tell me, do you advertise your practice?
210	A:	Somewhat. I take out ads, discreetly of course, in the newspaper and such places.
211	Q:	You're in a business, aren't you Dr. Barrier?
212	A:	I'm a physician with a practice.
213	Q:	That's a business, isn't it? Committed as you are to the care of your patients, you're not
214		running a charity operation?
215	A:	No.
216	Q:	Finally, would you say that The Crenshaw Group has a thriving practice?
217	A:	They do very well, yes. It's a large group, needless to say.
218	Q:	They're a direct competitor with your five-member group, aren't they?
219	A:	In areas where we overlap, yes. I've already said that.
220		Mr. Warnock: Your witness.
221		
222		Examination by Ms. Hayes:
223		
224	Q:	Dr. Barrier, what did you learn from Ms. Courtland with regards to the service contract
225		between Twin Oaks and The Crenshaw Group?
226	A:	That Twin Oaks is footing the entire bill, and that no other hospital that co-sponsored
227		health fairs or events in this area gave their co-sponsors such a deal. It's unheard of.
228	Q:	Tell me, why did you turn down the health fair offer from Ms. Rinehart?
229	A:	Because not only did I object to it being conducted exclusively by one physicians' group,
230		I knew that she wasn't offering me a real deal.
231	Q:	What do you mean?
232	A:	It was illusory. She knew I couldn't accept it. I'm part of a five-member practice. We have
233		to see our patients on Saturdays and we take calls for each other. I couldn't afford to take
234		off six Saturdays a year without adequate compensation at the expense of my practice.
235		She knew that full well, and that's why she made me a token offer that bore no real risk of
236		acceptance.
237	Q:	When you spoke earlier about your referral patterns, what dictates where you refer your
238		patients?

239 A: I send my patients where they want to go, so to the hospital of their choice. As long as
240   I believe in the hospital, and think the particular patient will benefit from the care of that
241   hospital, then the referral is made. It's not a matter of my convenience, but theirs—my
242   patients'.
243 Ms. Hayes: No more questions.
244
245 (End of Deposition: 11:20 a.m., December 1, YR-1.)
246
247
248   Certificate of Stenographer
249
250 I, Dana Shapiro, certified stenographic reporter for the court, CSR No. 09876, do hereby certify
251 that I reported in Stenograph notes the foregoing proceedings, and that they have been edited by
252 me, or under my direction and the foregoing transcript contains a full, true, complete and accurate
253 transcript of the proceedings held in this matter, to the best of my knowledge. I further certify that
254 this transcript of the proceedings truly and correctly reflects the exhibits, if any, offered by the
255 respective parties.
256   In witness, I have subscribed my name on this 1st day of December, YR-1.
257
258   *Dana Shapiro*
259   Dana Shapiro

DEPOSITION EXHIBIT A

Twin Oaks Hospital
1510 Riparian Way,
Overland Park, Kansas 56788
Office of the Administrator

June 4, YR-1

Dr. David E. Barrier
Managing Partner
Overland Park Bone and Joint Clinic
2345 Rockingham Avenue
Overland Park, Kansas 56788

Dear Dr. Barrier:

You mentioned your interest in participating in Twin Oaks' community health fairs, to be conducted in future on a six-fair-per-year basis: January, March, May, July, September, and November of each calendar year.

Would you join us on each of the dates, at a prorated share of the fee to be paid? It's a nominal amount, of course, but something we all do in betterment of the population. We'd of course love to have you as part of the events. They are all-day affairs, as you know, and on Saturdays. Let me know if we can work something out.

If you have any questions, please do not hesitate to call.

Sincerely,

Rosemary Rinehart

Rosemary Rinehart
Hospital Administrator

1		Deposition of Julia B. Courtland
2		Office of Warnock and Bailey
3		Kansas City, Kansas, December 1, YR-1, 1:00 P.M.
4		
5	After having been sworn, Julia B. Courtland testified:
6		
7	Examination by Mr. Warnock:
8		
9	Q:	For the record, state your full name and age.
10	A:	Julia Baines Courtland. I'm forty years old.
11	Q:	Your address?
12	A:	412 Canterbury Close, #323, Overland Park, Kansas.
13	Q:	Have you ever been deposed before, Ms. Courtland?
14	A:	No, I haven't.
15	Q:	All right. For clarity's sake, a deposition, which you're about to give, is sworn testimony
16		that can be used in the court proceeding instituted under the False Claims Act
17		against your former employer, my client, Twin Oaks Hospital, by Dr. David Barrier.
18		Dr. Barrier is represented by Ms. Hayes. I'll ask you questions, then Ms. Hayes will
19		ask you questions. Your own attorney, Mr. Zachary, may object to questions asked
20		and Mr. Warnock might object too. The objections will be put into the record by the
21		court reporter and a judge will decide if your answer can be used at trial. Do you
22		understand that?
23	A:	Yes.
24	Q:	You came here today in response to a subpoena from the federal district court here in
25		Kansas City, correct?
26	A:	Yes.
27	Q:	And you've sworn to tell the truth today?
28	A:	Yes.
29	Q:	Do you have any qualifications about that oath?
30	A:	No.
31	Q:	Are you on any medication, stimulants, or drugs, or do you have any health problems that
32		would interfere with your testimony?
33	A:	No.
34	Q:	We can take a break any time you'd like. You just say so. All right?
35	A:	Yes.
36	Q:	If you don't understand a question, I'll rephrase it for you. Or if you didn't hear it, I'll be
37		glad to repeat it. Just ask.
38	A:	Okay.
39	Q:	Was there anything unclear about what I just told you?
40	A:	No. I understand.
41	Q:	So you can think of no reason why you cannot give full and accurate testimony here
42		today?
43	A:	No.
44	Q:	All right. Ms. Courtland, you were formally an employee of Twin Oaks Hospital in Overland
45		Park, correct?
46	A.	Yes.
47	Q:	And what was your position there?
48	A:	I was the Director of Hospital Services from January 1, YR-7 to July 31, YR-1.
49	Q:	And to whom did you report?
50	A:	To Ms. Rinehart, the Hospital Administrator.
51	Q:	You're currently employed by Overland Park Regional Hospital, isn't that so?
52	A:	Yes, in a similar position.
53	Q:	What were your duties while at Twin Oaks?
54	A:	I was in charge of affairs within the hospital, that is, the staff and our relations with
55		hospital patrons.
56	Q:	You resigned that position, did you not?
57	A:	I did.
58	Q:	You stated in your resignation letter to Ms. Rinehart, dated July 15, YR-1, that you felt
59		your talents would be better employed elsewhere, considering the hospital's staffing choices
60		of late?

61	A:	Yes.
62	Q:	You gave no other reason at that time?
63	A:	No, but she knew I was displeased with the way I was treated.
64	Q:	But just to be clear, you say she knew, though you never wrote to her or stated your
65		grievances in any formal way prior to that time?
66	A:	No, not in any formal, written way. But I spoke of the long work hours they were
67		demanding of me, and of the job being larger than the compensation justified. I didn't
68		see why my job was being expanded to include things that should be part of another
69		department. I also objected to what I saw as outside influence having a negative effect on
70		our staff.
71	Q:	Just before your resignation, you failed to win a post as Public Relations Director with the
72		hospital, isn't that correct?
73	A:	Yes, and I believe one of the reasons I failed to receive that position, though qualified for it,
74		was due to criticisms voiced by Dr. Andrew Crenshaw.
75	Q:	Ms. Courtland, the Public Relations position was advertised as requiring a degree in
76		journalism. You don't have that degree, do you?
77	A:	No, but I have many years of practical experience and was a known commodity.
78	Q:	The position was filled by an applicant not only with that degree, but with a masters degree
79		in business, were you aware of that?
80	A:	I was. But the hospital has always advanced the careers of inside hires as an unstated
81		policy. It's not uncommon for them to advertise one way and hire another. Last year, a
82		longtime employee, Jim Farrington, was tapped to head the Payroll department, though he
83		didn't have the degree stated in the job advertisement. Plus, my co-workers all assured me
84		I was a shoe-in, and that seemed the case up until so much criticism was directed my way
85		by Dr. Crenshaw.
86	Q:	You never received assurances from Ms. Rinehart to that effect, did you? Not from her or
87		any of her staff?
88	A:	No. I wouldn't have expected to either. Protocols had to be observed.
89	Q:	Ms. Courtland, one of your duties during that time was to plan and implement a series of
90		health fairs for Twin Oaks?
91	A.	Yes. I was asked to take on that job, though it was not within my job description and no
92		one could explain why it was given to me to do. It should've been done by the Director of
93		Business Development's office, not mine.
94	Q:	How many years did you administrate that task?
95	A:	From YR-3, when we started them, until just last year. So I was in charge for two years
96		before they were outsourced to The Crenshaw Group.
97	Q:	In a staff meeting in September of YR-2, you stated that you were overwhelmed by the
98		responsibility of the fairs, didn't you Ms. Courtland?
99	A:	I said all of my duties were overwhelming me. I was being given more to do than I could do
100		in a responsible way. My current employers understand that completely. I have twice the
101		size staff than I had at Twin Oaks.
102	Q:	The attendance numbers at the fairs, as reported on the hospital's website, have doubled
103		since The Crenshaw Group took over. How do you explain that, Ms. Courtland?
104	A:	They've doubled the budget and staff resources for it, that's why. And they've doubled the
105		number of fairs since Dr. Crenshaw and five of his partners have begun to be paid to do
106		what we did in-house before. They're much more elaborate things than they were.
107	Q:	If the fairs are more elaborate, why is that not a reflection on your own complacency?
108	Mr. Zachary:	Objection. That's an accusation, not a question.
109	Mr. Warnock:	I'll withdraw that and ask instead if it's not true that Ms. Rinehart requested that
110		you put more effort into the fairs before the hospital entered into a service contract
111		with The Crenshaw Group?
112	A:	She did. But it was becoming absurd, frankly. I'd put an enormous deal of effort into the
113		fairs already, with a very limited staff. As I said, my job duties were creeping up to an
114		unmanageable degree. I couldn't do everything, and was being stretched too thin, especially
115		considering the salary I was being paid. She didn't seem willing to hear it.
116	Q:	But despite your repeated complaints about having to oversee the fairs, you complained to
117		Ms. Rinehart about being relieved of that responsibility?
118	A:	I wouldn't have minded doing them if she'd given me the proper staff and budget, and
119		I was certainly shocked to be kept in the dark about her giving the fairs to The Crenshaw
120		Group.

121	Q:	Right after you resigned from Twin Oaks, you phoned the plaintiff, Dr. Barrier, on July 17
122		of last year concerning The Crenshaw Group's service contract with Twin Oaks, didn't you,
123		Ms. Courtland?
124	A:	Yes. He's a lifelong friend.
125	Q:	You were in a staff meeting when you learned the information about that contract?
126	A:	I was. It was a staff meeting of all the department heads on February 1, YR-1. The Chief
127		Financial Officer, Barry Farr, asked Ms. Rinehart whether Dr. Crenshaw had signed the
128		contract yet, and she said no. Then he said, "What's he got to lose, seeing as it's no cost to
129		them?"
130	Q:	Did Ms. Rinehart answer?
131	A:	No, she moved on to the meeting's agenda. But afterwards, I stopped Barry and asked him
132		what he meant by "no cost" and regarding what contract. He seemed to think I'd know what
133		he meant. He just said the hospital was footing the entire bill and staffing the entire thing
134		itself, for each of the fairs. That was the first I'd learned of the fairs being outsourced, and
135		outsourced for free to boot.
136	Q:	You just assumed that the compensation wasn't justified?
137	A:	I didn't assume anything. I just know that it's a deal no one else is getting. As part of
138		my job, I know what kinds of arrangements the hospitals have with their co-sponsors.
139		At Overland Park Regional, we co-sponsor fairs as well, but our co-sponsors share in the
140		expenses.
141	Q:	But these co-sponsors are listed as such in the advertisement and marketing, correct?
142	A:	Yes.
143	Q:	And Twin Oaks was and is the only sponsor of its health fairs, isn't that true?
144	A:	Yes, but considering the little amount of work that the Crenshaw Group did, and the
145		disproportionate amount of exposure they got, they were de facto co-sponsors.
146	Q:	That's just your opinion though, isn't it Ms. Courtland? Your assessment of what's just
147		compensation, without any knowledge of the arrangement's particulars?
148	A:	It's unheard of. That's an objective fact.
149	Q:	It's unheard of to you, but that doesn't make the arrangement improper, does it?
150	A:	It would be suspicious to anyone who knew anything about hospital services.
151	Q:	You were angry at the hospital at the time of that February 1st meeting, weren't you?
152	A:	I think it's understandable to be upset when you've learned about so many injustices, as
153		I have. If anything, it's righteous indignation.
154	Q:	So you feel you were justifiably angry when you called Dr. Barrier about The Crenshaw
155		Group's contract?
156	A:	Yes.
157		Mr. Warnock: No further questions.
158		
159		Examination by Ms. Hayes:
160		
161	Q:	You say the health fairs became more elaborate after The Crenshaw Group got the contract
162		to oversee them. How?
163	A:	Oh, they spent much more money on food and began to pay for transportation, running
164		shuttles by designated places to pick up senior citizens. They advertised in markets that
165		would appeal to that audience—something they never asked me to do. They never gave
166		me the budget to do those things. They must've doubled the budget, in fact. They even
167		put together a website and a sign-up sheet for transportation requests. The staff they put
168		behind the fairs was doubled too. I was running the things with a skeleton crew, exhausting
169		myself. Despite my complaints, I got no extra help.
170	Q:	Had past attendees ever complained of the fairs' quality?
171	A:	Just the opposite. We were given high marks on the surveys we distributed. And seeing as
172		they were on the hospital's campus, we were praised for our facilities and people got to know
173		the place. Despite our disappointment at the support from the hospital administration, my
174		crew was proud of our work and none of us could understand why The Crenshaw Group was
175		asked to perform at a cost what we were doing for free.
176	Q:	You made a statement about Dr. Crenshaw's influence on your job application, as well as on
177		the staffing at the hospital. Could you elaborate there?
178	A:	He and I didn't get along. He was from a different time, and felt entitled to a great deal of
179		deference in matters from the hospital staff. We had several disagreements over the years

180   concerning how my staff should do their jobs. The problem was that Ms. Rinehart took his
181   side, deferring to him because of his importance.
182 Q: Importance?
183 A: His retirement facilities and his geriatric practice coincide with the interests of the
184   hospital.
185 Q: He criticized you directly?
186 A: He told Ms. Rinehart I was insubordinate. Dr. Crenshaw thought I wasn't responsive to
187   his requests for information about the fairs. For that, he let me know that he was going to
188   register his opinion about me to Ms. Rinehart, just before the job for which I was applying
189   got filled.
190 Q: When the contract was given to The Crenshaw Group, did you question the propriety of the
191   arrangement?
192 A: Yes. Right after she made her decision to relieve me of the fair duties, I approached
193   Ms. Rinehart and told her that she should seek advice about entering into a contract with a
194   group that referred so much business to the hospital. I've worked long enough in this area to
195   know what looks suspicious. I told her as much.
196 Q: Her reply?
197 A: She said that the hospital had a compliance officer, as I well knew, and that he would make
198   the call on whether such a step was necessary. That was the last I ever heard of it.
199 Ms. Hayes: Thank you. No further questions.
200
201 (End of Deposition: 1:40 p.m., December 1, YR-1.)
202
203   Certificate of Stenographer
204
205 I, Dana Shapiro, certified stenographic reporter for the court, CSR No. 09876, do hereby certify
206 that I reported in Stenograph notes the foregoing proceedings, and that they have been edited by
207 me, or under my direction and the foregoing transcript contains a full, true, complete and accurate
208 transcript of the proceedings held in this matter, to the best of my knowledge. I further certify that
209 this transcript of the proceedings truly and correctly reflects the exhibits, if any, offered by the
210 respective parties.
211   In witness, I have subscribed my name on this 1st day of December, YR-1.
212
213
214   *Dana Shapiro*
                              Dana Shapiro

1	Deposition of Rosemary Creighton Rinehart
2	Offices of Leland, Hayes, and Leland
3	Overland Park, Kansas, December 7, YR-1, 2:00 P.M.
4	
5	After having been sworn, Rosemary C. Rinehart testified:
6	
7	Examination by Ms. Hayes:
8	
9	Q: Please state your name and age for the record.
10	A: Rosemary Creighton Rinehart. I'm fifty-nine.
11	Q: Have you been deposed before, Ms. Rinehart?
12	A: Yes.
13	Q: As part of your job or for other reasons?
14	A: Both.
15	Q: How many times?
16	A: Three times. Twice involving the hospital and once involving a property dispute.
17	Q: So you're familiar with the process?
18	A: Yes.
19	Q: As you may recall, this testimony is sworn, and is subject to use in the lawsuit under
20	the False Claims Act brought by Dr. David Barrier against your employer, Twin Oaks
21	Hospital.
22	A: I understand that.
23	Q: And you have sworn to tell the truth? No qualms about that oath?
24	A: No qualms.
25	Q: I'll ask questions of you, and your attorney may object to those questions and will tell you
26	whether to answer or not. But those questions will nevertheless be part of the record for a
27	judge to decide upon. Everything is being taken down by the court reporter over there. You
28	understand?
29	A: Yes.
30	Q: Mr. Warnock may ask you some questions later, and then I can ask you more if necessary.
31	All right?
32	A: All right.
33	Q: You're under no medication or suffering from any illness that would prevent your
34	unqualified testimony today, is that right?
35	A: No.
36	Q: If you need a break we'll take one, but I think this will be a short deposition all in all.
37	There'll only be a few questions, at least from my end. If you need clarification on anything,
38	just ask me. Okay?
39	A: Okay.
40	Q: How long have you been the Hospital Administrator there at Twin Oaks?
41	A: At Twin Oaks, seven years.
42	A: And before that time?
43	Q: I was the administrator at a county hospital in Western Kansas for five years. Before
44	that, I was an assistant administrator at the same place for about fifteen. I've been in the
45	hospital administration field, in some capacity, my whole professional life.
46	Q: For all intents and purposes, a Hospital Administrator is the chief operating officer of a
47	hospital, isn't that right? In charge of running the entire outfit?
48	A: That's a fair assessment, yes.
49	Q: You answer to no one but the hospital board, correct?
50	A: Yes. That's the chain of command.
51	Q: How big is Twin Oaks Hospital, Ms. Rinehart?
52	A: We have 300 beds. We're going though an expansion next year to add another fifty.
53	Q: And the hospital's affiliation?
54	A: It's a private hospital, founded in the last century, philanthropically. It has no affiliation
55	with a school or religious group.
56	Q: Ms. Rinehart, Twin Oaks was the defendant in a separate, unrelated whistleblower suit
57	two years ago brought by another party involving leased equipment, correct?
58	A: Yes. That claim was settled without ramifications for the hospital.
59	Q; It was settled by agreement between the Hospital and the Department of Health and
60	Human Services dated March 15, YR-2, correct?

61 A: Yes. I believe that's the date.

62 Q: And as part of that settlement, the hospital agreed that HHS's payment of the hospital's
63   reimbursement claims was expressly conditional upon the hospital's compliance with all
64   federal statutes, including the federal False Claims Act and the federal Anti-Kickback
65   Statute.

66 A: Yes, we did agree to that and we've kept that promise.

67 Q: That settlement agreement was to run for a period of three years from March 15, YR-2,
68   which means it's still in effect. Isn't that right?

69 A: Yes.

70 Q: That kind of certification is not standard, is it Ms. Rinehart?

71 A: No, but we felt perfectly comfortable making that certification, as we've always complied
72   with the federal laws and we're doing so now. We have a compliance officer on staff that
73   makes sure of that fact.

74 Q: Ms. Rinehart, when was River Crest retirement community built?

75 A: Over the past few years, but it opened in January of YR-1.

76 Q: Its location?

77 A: About a mile down the road from us.

78 Q: And you receive a lot of patients from there?

79 A: Of course. It's close. And it's a large new facility, with a variety of living
80   arrangements—from nursing care to assisted living to independent homes and
81   townhouses. So the residents have many medical needs that must be met, and we're
82   glad to serve them.

83 Q: But the hospital has more than a geographical closeness to River Crest, doesn't it?
84   There's a business arrangement between River Crest and Twin Oaks, isn't there?

85 A: Well, we have an arrangement with The Crenshaw Group, which owns River Crest, if that's
86   what you're referring to.

87 Q: Yes, Twin Oaks' relationship with The Crenshaw Group. And for the record, that's the
88   partnership of doctors headed by Dr. Andrew Crenshaw, correct?

89 A: Yes.

90 Q: Let me ask you some questions about that relationship. The Crenshaw Group, they're
91   under contract with Twin Oaks to conduct health fairs at River Crest—in their Pavilion
92   Complex—isn't that so?

93 A: That's right. It's a large facility on their campus, in a park-like setting separate from the
94   residential areas. The complex can accommodate all kinds of events. In fact, we're lucky
95   to get the space. Civic groups have been renting it out a lot, and it's become a sought-after
96   venue.

97 Q: And again, these health fairs you conduct, they're overseen by The Crenshaw Group, isn't
98   that right?

99 A: Yes, that's right. We entered into that agreement last year.

100 Q: But you'd been conducting these health fairs for several years before then, hadn't you?

101 A: For two years before then, yes.

102 Q: Back then, they were conducted only three times a year, on the hospital campus, correct?

103 A: Yes, during the warmer months.

104 Q: And you conducted them yourself, by way of your own staff, during that time. Isn't that so?
105   With no outside help?

106 A: That's right.

107 Q: Julia Courtland, the director of your Hospital Services department—she and her staff were
108   in charge of the events up until then, were they not?

109 A: Yes. We decided to make a change.

110 Q: A change from in-house staff conducting the health fairs, as part of their jobs, to
111   outsourcing the events to The Crenshaw Group, under a paid contract?

112 A: Yes. It was our professional opinion that Ms. Courtland had become complacent about
113   performing her duties in that respect. She even complained of the trouble and budgetary
114   expense they caused and the extra work they were causing her. Since we felt these fairs
115   are an important part of our community outreach, we decided to take them in a different
116   direction, which she didn't like.

117 Q: Ms. Courtland expressed her confusion to you about the necessity of this joint venture,
118   didn't she?

119 Mr. Warnock: Objection. You're characterizing this as a joint venture. That's not established.

120	Ms. Hayes:	I'll rephrase. Ms. Courtland expressed her confusion about the necessity of this
121		arrangement, didn't she?
122	A:	Yes, she did. Ms. Courtland had many complaints about her job, in fact—ones she stated
123		publically in a staff meeting. She also resented not receiving a promotion to another position
124		that we filled with a more qualified outside hire. All that apparently led to her voluntary
125		resignation a few months ago. You'd have to ask her about that though.
126	Q:	Didn't she ask why you would give them to The Crenshaw Group by way of the Service
127		Contract dated February 28, YR-1, and why you would conduct the fairs at River Crest?
128	A:	She asked, and I told her that was our decision to make. Anyhow, the fairs were never to be
129		held exclusively at River Crest. Under the contract, there were to be six health fairs a year,
130		for the next five years, conducted at different locations. One at each of The Crenshaw Group
131		retirement facilities—they own three in the metropolitan area, one of which is River Crest—
132		and then three more at the convention center downtown.
133	Q:	But only two fairs were conducted last year, is that not correct? And both were at River
134		Crest?
135	A:	That was not by design, Ms. Hayes.
136	Q:	Nevertheless, three of the six fairs were always planned to be held at facilities owned by The
137		Crenshaw Group, correct?
138	A:	Yes, that's right. Since they were overseeing them, we thought that convenient. Of course,
139		these fairs are really only means by which we can keep our name visible in the community
140		and to perform a service for the population.
141	Q:	And also to drum up business?
142	A:	That's what we're in, Ms. Hayes. A business. And a very competitive one at that. These are
143		tough times in the health care field. Besides, the last time I checked, that's not illegal—to do
144		what you can to stay in business.
145	Q:	You and some of your senior staff attended the health fairs yourselves, didn't you?
146	A:	Yes. We were supportive.
147	Q:	But you never went to them in the past, did you?
148	A:	Well, no, but last year we decided they were something to get behind in a larger, more public
149		way. The ones in the summer months, in particular, became a priority, as they're the best
150		attended.
151	Q:	You doubled your expenses associated with the fairs, did you not? And there are three more
152		fairs now than there were when Ms. Courtland was in charge?
153	A:	Yes, as I said, we decided to forefront them in our community outreach campaign. Our
154		overall expenses for that campaign didn't increase, however. There was no greater outlay of
155		cash in our budget. We just redirected where we wanted to spend the money.
156	Q:	Ms. Rinehart, these fairs are aimed primarily at senior citizens, aren't they?
157	A:	No, I wouldn't say so.
158	Q:	But looking at your own literature and webpage regarding the event, they involved blood
159		pressure screening, cholesterol screening, lectures on hypertension and nutrition and
160		mobility seminars, among other things.
161	A:	Those aren't concerns that relate exclusively to senior citizens.
162	Q:	Then why were half of the fairs scheduled to occur at retirement facilities, Ms. Rinehart?
163	A:	As I said, the Pavilion at River Crest is popular. It's separate from the residential area, in
164		a park-like area with a separate entrance. It's been used by all kinds of civic groups since
165		it opened. And it's only a mile down the road from us. As to the other two events at The
166		Crenshaw Group facilities, since they were overseeing the fairs, we thought it would be
167		convenient for them as well. They're a multi-specialty practice group that sees all kinds of
168		patients and we didn't want things to be too hard for them accommodation-wise.
169	Q:	But The Crenshaw Group's specialties happen to coincide with the needs of the large senior
170		citizen population in the area, many of which reside in the three retirement facilities that
171		they own, isn't that right?
172	Mr. Warnock:	Objection. That's not a question. That's an accusation. She shouldn't have to
173		answer that.
174	Q:	All right. I'll withdraw it. Now, Ms. Rinehart, the fairs were well attended, weren't they?
175	A:	In the summer months they were very well attended. Fewer came when the weather got
176		bad, but there was always a respectable showing.
177	Q:	There was a charge for attendance at these fairs, wasn't there?
178	A:	Yes, a nominal one. The cost was subsidized by us for the most part.
179	Q:	But senior citizens were discounted even more, weren't they?

180 A: Yes. But most live on fixed incomes, and we thought that was appropriate. Besides, the
181   purpose of these fairs is not only to provide information to the attendees, but also to develop
182   a rapport with them. Hopefully, when they or their families have a choice of health care
183   providers, we come to mind.
184 Q: You provided free transportation to these events for senior citizens, did you not? By way of
185   shuttles that ran throughout the area?
186 A: Yes.
187 Q: They went by designated local churches, retirement communities—ones not owned by The
188   Crenshaw Group—and several other designated locations all day long, picking up people to
189   bring to the fairs. That was the arrangement?
190 A: That's right. They could come on our website and sign up for the shuttles.
191 Q: You even advertised the fairs in local publications and websites aimed at the elderly, so
192   they'd know where to catch the shuttle, isn't that so?
193 A: Yes, we wanted them to come.
194 Q: But if these events weren't aimed at the senior citizens, why did you provide free
195   transportation to them alone?
196 A: Ms. Hayes, we obviously wanted to make it possible for them to attend. They were the
197   only population that might not be able to come if they thought getting to the event was
198   complicated. As I said before, the fairs weren't designed to appeal exclusively to the elderly,
199   but they were indeed a target audience.
200 Q: And can you explain why you asked The Crenshaw Group in particular to run these health
201   fairs?
202 A: Well, again, the Pavilion is close by. It's a popular location and everyone knows where it is.
203   And since The Crenshaw Group owns the facility, and it's comprised of doctors that are well-
204   respected members of our staff, it was a natural choice. They were glad to do it. You can ask
205   Dr. Crenshaw himself.
206 Q: What are they paid under that contract?
207 A: A nominal fee—just something for their trouble, as only about five doctors were to
208   participate during the six events. Twenty-five-thousand dollars for the whole five years. It's
209   really a donation of their time and space, considering that the rental of the Pavilion for the
210   six days is not much less than that. But they see it as part of their community service, just
211   as we do.
212 Q: But your own hospital goes to considerable expense to run these fairs—to provide
213   entertainment and transportation, along with the health-related events, isn't that so?
214 A: It's an expense, yes, but one worth the investment in goodwill.
215 Q: You also provide the staff to run the events, isn't that right?
216 A: Yes, we staff it ourselves. That's to be expected.
217 Q: The large elderly population in the area—the one that you go to such expense to attract to
218   these fairs—they're potential patients of The Crenshaw Group, are they not?
219 A: Potentially. But at danger of repeating myself, The Crenshaw Group is not a charity and
220   neither are we. The Crenshaw Group hopes to attract patients, as do we. I fail to see why
221   that's a surprise to anyone.
222 Ms. Hayes: Let the record show that I am now handing the court reporter a letter dated July 1,
223   YR-1, written on the stationery of Twin Oaks Hospital, Office of the Hospital
224   Administrator. I ask that the letter be designated Deposition "Exhibit A."
225 (The exhibit is marked)
226   I'm now handing the witness that same piece of stationery. Do you recognize this letter,
227 Ms. Rinehart?
228 A: Yes. I wrote it.
229 Q: And it's addressed to Dr. Andrew Crenshaw, managing partner of The Crenshaw Group,
230   correct?
231 A: Yes.
232 Q: It bears your signature, correct?
233 A: It does.
234 Q: What's the purpose of that letter, Ms. Rinehart?
235 A: Dr. Crenshaw had complained of the staff at the health fairs, the staff that we supplied.
236   Some of them were being insolent and unhelpful to him. I suppose they were resentful
237   that The Crenshaw Group was now in charge. I wanted to assure him such behavior
238   would not be countenanced and said that any recommendations of his would be given top
239   priority.

240 Q: Ms. Rinehart, can you read the second paragraph aloud?
241 A: The second paragraph?
242 Q: Yes, just read it aloud. The court reporter will record the statement.
243 A: "This measure is the least we can do for a group with such a large geriatric practice,
244   which is so important to us both. Again, our staff is a reflection upon us, so any
245   suggestions or comment you make as to the composition of that staff will be valued and
246   acted upon."
247 Q: Thank you. Now, tell me, Ms. Rinehart, the measure you're referring to there about the
248   staff, which you state is being offered because of the size of the lessee's geriatric practice—
249   you're referring to Ms. Courtland and her staff aren't you?
250 A: Yes. They were not doing what I asked them to do. That's the reason for the letter. In the
251   passage you're referring to, I'm simply identifying the lessee with regard to its practice area,
252   and that the senior citizen population is important to us both. That's all.
253 Q: So you give Dr. Crenshaw a voice in staffing matters in general at your hospital because of
254   his geriatric practice?
255 A: No. We were unhappy about our end of the bargain and we wanted to make it right. That
256   was just the honest thing to do. I was simply saying that I valued their input, just as I do
257   that of all our physicians.
258 Q: But have you sent such a letter deferring authority with regard to any other matter?
259 A: That's not what it is—a deferral of authority. These are health fairs that have as a central—
260   though certainly not exclusive—focus. The elderly population. That is a central, though
261   certainly not exclusive, focus of The Crenshaw Group as well. I wanted them to be happy
262   and know that I valued their concerns. That's good business. Nothing else.
263 Q: You admit that The Crenshaw Group is a special concern of yours.
264 A: Their reputation is known in this area. Their business is much sought after. We felt lucky
265   to have them involved in this community outreach effort. To lose them because of our staff's
266   rudeness would be a blow.
267 Q: To lose their business, the source of their referrals, you mean?
268 A: To lose their business, period, I mean.
269 Q: Neither Dr. Barrier or any other group received such a voice in staffing, did they?
270 A: Dr. Barrier was offered a chance to come onto the staff of the fairs early on. He refused
271   because of the size of his practice. If he regrets his choice, I can understand that. But I don't
272   see why we're responsible for his bad business decisions.
273 Q: Ms. Rinehart, Dr. Barrier has filed this suit because he believes the relationship between
274   Twin Oaks Hospital and The Crenshaw Group is improper, running afoul of the federal
275   Anti-Kickback statute. It's typical for health care providers to seek an advisory opinion
276   from the Health and Human Services Department regarding business arrangements—
277   particularly service contracts—that they enter into with those who can potentially refer
278   patients whose expenses are reimbursable through government funds. Now, did you ever
279   seek such an opinion from HHS, Ms. Rinehart?
280 A: The propriety of the service contract was never in question, as far as I was concerned. Why
281   would I seek guidance about a contract that for all intents and purposes is a formality—
282   being that no one makes any money on it? It simply memorializes a means fostering
283   goodwill in the community. Besides, we strive to meet all of the safe harbors in this area
284   and even have a compliance officer, Dan Webster, who oversees our conformance with them.
285   I take his advice on such matters, which I did on this one.
286 Q: You asked him specifically about this matter?
287 A: I asked him in theory whether this was something we should seek advice about, but he
288   wasn't overly concerned about it.
289 Q: So the answer is no, then? You did not seek such an opinion from HHS?
290 A: The answer is no. However, I've asked his opinion about other matters and he's
291   recommended we seek an HHS opinion after conferring with independent consultants.
292   I followed that advice in the past. He didn't recommend getting an opinion here, so I didn't.
293   There's no point in having a compliance officer if you don't trust his advice.
294 Q: Ms. Rinehart, what is the sum of your total yearly Medicare reimbursements, on average?
295 A: I couldn't say precisely. I'd have to look that up.
296 Q: Could you estimate?
297 Mr. Warnock: Objection. She can't speculate on that. She's not prepared to answer a question on
298 such matters in detail.
299 Ms. Hayes: An estimate is fine. I'm just after a rough percentage.

300	A:	Well, I'd estimate around forty-five percent.
301	Q:	And of that figure, your estimate as to what percentage is attributable to referrals from The
302		Crenshaw Group?
303	A:	Again, I'd have to look up a precise figure. But perhaps twenty-five percent.
304	Q:	It would be fair to say that the better The Crenshaw Group's business, the more referrals
305		you receive?
306	A:	All I can do is repeat myself. It should be no surprise that we seek referrals. We do nothing
307		to seek them dishonestly. In addition to Dan Webster, our internal compliance officer,
308		we even have yearly audits by independent compliance consultants regarding our lease
309		agreements, to ensure conformity with the Settlement Agreement.
310	Q:	But those compliance consultants focus only on your leases, correct? They don't look at
311		service contracts, right? They didn't look at this service contract in particular, did they?
312	A:	Of course not. No one made money on it. We've had no cause for its review.
313	Ms. Hayes: Your witness	
314		
315	Examination of Mr. Warnock	
316	Q:	You spoke of tough times. What are you referring to in particular?
317	A:	Well, this is a very competitive market—health care in a big metropolitan area like this has
318		many players. Obviously, we're not the only hospital in the vicinity. At least three others,
319		just as close to The Crenshaw Group's two other retirement communities as we are to River
320		Crest, want their business. They were courting the group when the news got around that it
321		needed more space for its practice. Those hospitals wanted to have The Crenshaw Group in
322		their office buildings—something we don't have. On top of that, White Cross Corporation, of
323		which I'm sure you're aware, is a national chain of health care providers. Even as we speak,
324		it's seeking to put a large Imaging Center—which conducts diagnostic scans—in direct
325		competition with us, only a block away from River Crest. There's a very large baby boomer,
326		retirement-age population in this area. White Cross has obviously done its research and
327		wants the referrals that are currently being sent to us. So we thought that getting—and
328		keeping—The Crenshaw Group in a close relationship would provide some level of security.
329		That's just good business, which as I've said, we have to be smart about if we hope to
330		survive.
331	Q:	Why were the only two fairs held last year at River Crest, Ms. Rinehart?
332	A:	The first fair was conducted in May, YR-1 at River Crest, as scheduled, and the second, in
333		July, had to be moved there from one of The Crenshaw Group's other facilities because of
334		inclement weather. The Pavilion is inside of course and the other place was set up for an
335		outside event. The third event, at the civic center downtown, had to be rescheduled because
336		of some issues they had with the cooling system in September, which was totally out of our
337		control. Then, before we could see to that, we learned of this lawsuit. The other fairs have
338		been put on hold, which is a shame, but something we thought prudent considering the
339		circumstances of Dr. Barrier's lawsuit.
340	Q:	Aren't events such as these health fairs typically within the job description of the Business
341		Development Director?
342	A:	Yes, but our Business Development Director has been stretched so thin with other tasks
343		that we thought it was a good chance to utilize Ms. Courtland's talents in that respect.
344		Unfortunately, she seemed to resent the responsibility.
345	Q:	Tell me about the hospital. What kind of reputation does it have?
346	A:	A great reputation. We've been designated a Hospital of Excellence with regard to all our
347		patient care and diagnostic capabilities by Quality First Benchmarking, a company that
348		reviews data on all hospitals and by a benchmarking survey that canvases local doctors on
349		their opinions.
350	Q:	In your opinion, why would The Crenshaw Group send you so many of its Medicare
351		patients?
352	A:	Well, for a variety of reasons. We're not only close by, but we've got the best reputation
353		in the metropolitan area—I'd even say in the state—for client satisfaction, particularly
354		with the elderly. We've made it one of our hallmarks, to provide the kind of patient
355		satisfaction and personalized attention that not only makes such a population feel
356		comfortable, but also keeps the families of such patients satisfied with the treatment
357		afforded. The accolades we've received reflect our success, in no small part owing to these
358		standards. Our facilities also draw high marks in that context—again, the best reputation
359		in the area.

360 Q: What do you mean about your facilities? How are they attractive to the elderly population
361 here in the area?
362 A: That, too, is one of our hallmarks. We provide onsite and offsite support for senior citizens
363 by way of counseling and seminars, a state-of-the-art physical therapy center—also
364 benchmarked as one of the best in the country—a gym with a track and with mobility
365 classes devoted to senior citizens, at very affordable rates. There's also a café—just a variety
366 of things that make us popular with that group, who often complain that they're neglected
367 by society in general, let alone by the medical industry. We're proud of the good reputation
368 we've fostered.
369 Q: Finally, you're related to one of the physicians in The Crenshaw Group, isn't that correct,
370 Ms. Rinehart?
371 A: Yes. My brother is Dr. Clark Milner, an orthopedic surgeon there. I don't think there's any
372 harm in saying that I exercise whatever influence I can have over my brother as far as
373 selling him on the kind of hospital we have.
374 Mr. Warnock: Thank you. That's all. No further questions.
375
376 (End of Deposition: 2:45 p.m., December 7, YR-1.)
377
378 Certificate of Stenographer
379
380 I, Alex Bancroft, certified stenographic reporter for the court, CSR No. 8765, do hereby certify that
381 I reported in Stenograph notes the foregoing proceedings, and that they have been edited by me,
382 or under my direction and the foregoing transcript contains a full, true, complete and accurate
383 transcript of the proceedings held in this matter, to the best of my knowledge. I further certify
384 that this transcript of the proceedings truly and correctly reflects the exhibits, if any, offered by
385 the respective parties.
386 In witness, I have subscribed my name on this 7th day of December, YR-1.
387
388 *Alex Bancroft*
389 Alex Bancroft

DEPOSITION EXHIBIT A

Twin Oaks Hospital
1510 Riparian Way,
Overland Park, Kansas 56788
Office of the Administrator

July 1, YR-1

Dr. Andrew Crenshaw
Managing Partner
The Crenshaw Group, LLP
Overland Park Medical Plaza
3500 Riparian Way
Overland Park, Kansas 56788

Dear Dr. Crenshaw:

Over the past several months, you've expressed your concerns with the adequacy of the staff we provide for the Twin Oaks Hospital Health Fairs. I want to assure you that those concerns, which are troubling not only as to their extent, but also as to their persistence, are a profound concern of mine as well. Please let me know how you want to address this matter and I will see that it's done.

This measure is the least we can do for a group with such a large geriatric practice, which is so important to us both. Our staff is a reflection upon us, so any suggestions or comments you make as to the composition of that staff will be valued and acted upon.

Sincerely,

Rosemary Rinehart

Rosemary Rinehart
Hospital Administrator

1		Deposition of Andrew M. Crenshaw, M.D.
2		Offices of Leland, Hayes, and Leland
3		Overland Park, Kansas, December 7, YR-1, 4:00 P.M.
4		
5	After having been sworn, Andrew M. Crenshaw testified:	
6		
7	Examination by Ms. Hayes:	
8		
9	Q:	Would you state your name for the record?
10	A:	Andrew Mooreland Crenshaw.
11	Q:	Your address?
12	A:	2578 Auckland Boulevard, Overland Park, Kansas.
13	Q:	And your profession?
14	A:	I'm an orthopedic surgeon, though I seldom perform surgery anymore. I spend most of my
15		time managing the medical practice that I founded here in Overland Park.
16	Q:	That's The Crenshaw Group, correct?
17	A:	Yes.
18	Q:	Your age?
19	A:	Sixty-One.
20	Q:	Have you ever been deposed before?
21	A:	No. This is my first time.
22	Q:	Then let me explain some things. The nature of this meeting is to take testimony for the
23		court proceedings initiated by my client, Dr. David Barrier, against Twin Oaks Hospital,
24		for violation of the federal False Claims Act. I'll ask you questions, then the hospital's
25		attorney, Mr. Warnock, will ask you questions. Your own attorney, Mr. Massey, might object
26		to questions asked and Mr. Warnock might object too. The objections will be put into the
27		record by the court reporter and a judge will decide if your answer can be used at trial. Do
28		you understand that?
29	A:	Yes.
30	Q:	I can ask you more questions, as can Mr. Warnock, in order. The questions and answers will
31		be recorded by the court reporter there. Do you understand?
32	A:	Yes.
33	Q:	You came here today in response to a subpoena, is that so? Issued by the district court?
34	A:	Yes.
35	Q:	And you understand that you have sworn to tell the truth here today?
36	A:	Yes.
37	Q:	Do you have any reservations about that oath?
38	A:	No.
39	Q:	Are you on any medication, stimulants, or drugs, or do you have any health problems that
40		would interfere with your testimony today?
41	A:	No.
42	Q:	No health problems?
43	A:	Not that I know of.
44	Q:	If you decide during questioning that you'd like to take a break, we'll do that, all right?
45	A:	Okay.
46	Q:	If you don't understand a question, you have a right to, and should ask for, clarification. Is
47		that understood?
48	A:	Yes.
49	Q:	If you need me to repeat a question, you just ask, and if you want to volunteer a clearer
50		answer than you gave to a previous question, just say so.
51	A:	All right.
52	Q:	Was there anything unclear about what I just told you?
53	A:	No. I understand.
54	Q:	So you can think of no reason why you cannot give full and accurate testimony here
55		today?
56	A:	No.
57	Q:	All right, then. Dr. Crenshaw, you have a large group of physicians in your practice, don't
58		you? Thirty-five in all?
59	A:	Yes, thirty-five.
60	Q:	And the practice areas? Could you name them?

61	A:	Well, we have orthopedic surgeons—that's how we started out—orthopedic surgery was our
62		only focus until about five years ago, when we diversified. So in addition to the orthopedic
63		surgeons, we have internists, ENTs—
64	Q:	Excuse me, what are "ENTs"?
65	A:	Oh—"Ear, Nose, and Throat" specialists.
66	Q:	I see. Go ahead. You were saying?
67	A:	Let's see—ophthalmologists, cardiologists, thoracic surgeons—I may have forgotten
68		something, but I believe that's it.
69	Q:	And you also have a large supporting staff as well, nurses, therapists—that kind of thing.
70	A:	We have the size staff necessary to treat our patients.
71	Q:	Now, Dr. Crenshaw, your group owns three retirement communities in the metropolitan
72		area, doesn't it?
73	A:	Yes.
74	Q:	Their names and locations vis-à-vis Twin Oaks?
75	A:	Well, River Crest, which is a mile away from Twin Oaks Hospital. And then there's Bluff
76		View and Valley Terrace, which are both on the other side of town. Valley Terrace is the
77		furthest away from Twin Oaks.
78	Q:	Are all the same size?
79	A:	Roughly, yes.
80	Q:	And all of these communities are basically the same in concept? With various living
81		arrangements, all the way from independent living to full-time nursing care?
82	A:	Yes.
83	Q:	Now, according to your website, Dr. Crenshaw, your multi-specialty practice is meant to
84		provide the total spectrum of care to your patients. A kind of "one-stop" medical practice,
85		isn't that so?
86	A:	Yes, that was the idea when we went in that direction. A good way to build a strong
87		patient base, in my view, is to make things convenient for them. Everything under one
88		roof, as it were. That way, people can get comfortable with a setting, a standard of care,
89		a staff, etc. They're loyal to something that has served them in the past, even when
90		new circumstances arise—a person who has a knee injury and has a good treatment
91		experience at our group is likely to return to us for other medical needs that present
92		themselves in the future. He can ask his surgeon who he should see about X, Y, or Z and
93		be given a name right down the hall, instead of a person miles away and with whom the
94		patient is unfamiliar. That was the business plan I set us on five years ago, and it's been a
95		successful one, in my opinion.
96	Q:	But Dr. Crenshaw, your primary focus is geriatric patients, isn't it—older patients who are
97		likely to be on Medicare? Your website says that's the case.
98	A:	No, our website says that geriatric needs are one of the things we are particularly
99		specialized in. That population is the least likely to tolerate change, or complication, and
100		appreciates the simplicity of one group serving all their needs. It's one of our specialties,
101		yes, but it is not at all as you characterize it. It's not our primary focus.
102	Q:	But how much of your yearly business involves Medicare referrals, on the average,
103		Dr. Crenshaw?
104		Mr. Massey: Objection. He's not prepared to answer that.
105		Ms. Hayes: Just a rough estimate then?
106		Mr. Massey: With the stipulation that he is only guessing, as he's not prepared.
107		Ms. Hayes: Agreed. Dr. Crenshaw?
108	A:	Oh, I don't know—maybe sixty percent.
109	Q;	And of that percentage, how many are River Crest residents when they require hospital
110		care?
111		Mr. Massey: Objection. He's not prepared to answer that either.
112		Ms. Hayes: Same stipulation as before? A rough estimate?
113		Mr. Massey: All right.
114	A:	Again, I guess around twenty-five percent.
115	Q:	I assume your physicians have privileges at all the major hospitals in the area?
116	A:	They do.
117	Q:	Are River Crest patients ever sent anywhere else?
118	A:	Rarely. It's only a mile down the road from Twin Oaks. Plus, Twin Oaks has the best
119		hospital when it comes to geriatric needs. That's the considered opinion of our staff.

120	Q:	And what percentage of the yearly average figure of Medicare referrals come from the other
121		two facilities, Bluff View and Valley Terrace?
122	A:	What percentage of our referrals to Twin Oaks come from those places? Is that what you're
123		asking?
124	Q:	Yes. With the same stipulation as to rough percentages, Mr. Massey.
125	A:	I suppose ten percent, total, from Bluff View and Valley Terrace.
126	Q:	So in addition to the twenty-five percent of patients referred to Twin Oaks from River
127		Crest, another ten percent of the Medicare referrals to Twin Oaks Hospital come from these
128		communities on the other side of town?
129	A:	That's attributable to the fact that Twin Oaks is the premier hospital for geriatrics, in our
130		professional opinion. Plus, patients' families have a say in where they want folks sent. It's
131		not all up to us.
132	Q:	Has the amount of referrals to Twin Oaks gone up over the past year, Dr. Crenshaw?
133	A:	Well, obviously it has, seeing as River Crest just opened in the last year. That would be a
134		natural consequence.
135	Q:	But have your referrals to Twin Oaks from the other two retirement communities—Bluff
136		View and Valley Terrace—gone up as well?
137	A:	Yes. They've gone up. As I mentioned, there are a lot of reasons to explain that.
138	Q:	Let's talk about the service contract The Crenshaw Group has with Twin Oaks Hospital
139		dated February 28, YR-1. Last year was your first to take on the responsibilities of that
140		five-year deal, wasn't it?
141	A:	Yes.
142	Q:	Had you participated in the health fairs before this agreement?
143	A:	Not me, personally. Some of the other physicians in my group might have. But the hospital
144		used to run these fairs itself in the past.
145	Q:	Correct me if I'm wrong, but under that contract, you're to stage health fairs at your
146		facilities three times a year, with up to five physicians overseeing the events. Then your
147		group oversees three other health fairs at the civic center downtown. Is that about it?
148	A:	Yes. But there were only two last year, both at River Crest, because of unforeseen
149		circumstances.
150	Q:	The hospital pays the staff that works at these fairs, and they pay for all food,
151		entertainment, transportation, and other expenses, correct?
152	A:	Yes.
153	Q:	Your participating physicians' duties are limited to speaking? An hour each at most?
154	A:	Yes, and general oversight.
155	Q:	Dr. Crenshaw, isn't it true that the vast majority of the attendees at these fairs are senior
156		citizens?
157	A:	I don't know. A large number of them happen to be, perhaps. But the fairs aren't advertised
158		as being for them alone.
159	Q:	Isn't it true that the residents of your three retirement facilities are major attendees?
160	A:	I can't say. Of course, the two we've had were at River Crest, so naturally a lot of those
161		residents would come. As to the other two places, the residents there could pick up the
162		shuttle and be driven over, I believe. The hospital helps out in that way, so I wouldn't be
163		surprised.
164	Q:	The records show around two hundred people with addresses from your communities, or
165		people who say they came with one of your residents.
166	A:	Well? I don't see why that matters.
167	Q:	How many of the attendees who aren't residents at your facilities became patients of yours
168		afterwards, Dr. Crenshaw?
169	A:	I don't know. I hope a lot of them did. What do you expect me to say?
170	Q:	You concede that the objective was to get new patients from these fairs?
171	A:	Well, our objective was to do something beneficial for the community as well as for
172		ourselves. I think that's a normal hope. You can be cynical about anything if you want to.
173	Q:	Conservatively speaking, would you hope to generate about five to ten percent of new
174		business from these fairs, Dr. Crenshaw?
175	A:	I'd hope to generate as much as possible, Ms. Hayes.
176	Q:	And this new business would consist of potential Medicare referrals to some hospital,
177		wouldn't it?
178	A:	We charge our patients, Ms. Hayes. And if they have to go to the hospital, the hospital
179		charges them, too. We stay in practice by providing excellent service to our patients, who

180	pay us by means of whatever health care arrangements they've made. I suspect that your
181	law firm does things in just the same way.
182	Ms. Hayes: No further questions. However, I would like to enter the website information of
183	Jackson County Transit Authority from YR-1 as Deposition Exhibit A, the city
184	website information as to scheduled health fairs, dated January 1, YR-1 as
185	Deposition Exhibit B, and the website information regarding shuttle service to
186	Twin Oaks Hospital's health fairs in YR-1 as Deposition Exhibit C.
187	
188	(the exhibits are marked)
189	
190	Ms. Hayes: Your witness, Mr. Warnock.
191	
192	Examination by Mr. Warnock:
193	
194	Q: The Crenshaw Group's compensation under the service contract isn't equivalent to the
195	rental space for the Pavilion, is it Dr. Crenshaw?
196	A: Hardly. For six Saturdays a year for five years, that space would be rented at many times
197	the amount we're paid under that contract. But we effectively donate it along with our time.
198	We think these fairs are important, serving the community at large. If we create goodwill
199	through them, then all the better. As far as I know, that's not something the government
200	outlaws. At least not yet.
201	Q: Tell me about the staffing problems at the fairs.
202	A: We wanted a say as to the staff working there, as there were some inadequate responses
203	given to us when we complained about the problems, and frankly, some outright rudeness
204	from Julia Courtland. The hospital agreed with us on that.
205	Q: When you decided to enter into this agreement, were you considering other options?
206	A: Of course. All of the other hospitals in the area have them and they court us as well. They
207	still are, as a matter of fact. I was contacted by a leasing agent from St. Michael's just the
208	other day, trying to sell me on a space they've opened up in a building right beside their
209	hospital. And Overland Park Regional Hospital calls me often trying to lure us over there.
210	Q: You said Twin Oaks has a reputation for great geriatric care. Can you elaborate on that?
211	A: Well, for one thing, their patient satisfaction is the best. They're known for that. In fact,
212	they're nationally recognized for it. Time and again, patients—particularly those who
213	are often neglected because of their age—have commented on the extent of attention and
214	responsiveness they receive there. In addition, the turnover of beds and the scheduling is
215	top-notch at Twin Oaks. A doctor isn't always being told that there's no room, or that he
216	or she has to schedule surgery late in the afternoon because the hospital is flooded with
217	surgical procedures. They can handle the amount of work they have because they run
218	the place efficiently. They also have a state-of-the-art physical therapy center, plus a gym
219	complex that patients like. It's just very well done. Now, other hospitals are getting in on the
220	act, I must say. Their competitors haven't been sleeping. They know what patients like and
221	are fighting to put in the same facilities. Things change quickly in this area.
222	Mr. Warnock: No further questions.
223	
224	(End of Deposition: 4:45 p.m., December 7, YR-1.)
225	
226	Certificate of Stenographer
227	
228	I, Alex Bancroft, certified stenographic reporter for the court, CSR No. 8765, do hereby certify that
229	I reported in Stenograph notes the foregoing proceedings, and that they have been edited by me,
230	or under my direction and the foregoing transcript contains a full, true, complete and accurate
231	transcript of the proceedings held in this matter, to the best of my knowledge. I further certify
232	that this transcript of the proceedings truly and correctly reflects the exhibits, if any, offered by
233	the respective parties.
234	In witness, I have subscribed my name on this 7th day of December, YR-1.
235	
236	*Alex Bancroft*
237	Alex Bancroft

DEPOSITION EXHIBIT A

Website address: http: www.JCTA/Mobility.com/YR-1

Johnson County Transit Authority:

- JCTA prides itself on the number of bus lines and routes serving the Kansas City Metropolitan Area. We have won national recognition for our mobility initiatives, which provide special rates for senior citizens (flat rates of $3.00/one way system-wide), accessibility-friendly buses, and stops at all local civic and cultural venues in the greater metropolitan vicinity, including Overland Park, Shawnee, Prairie Village, Leawood, and Mission Hills.

DEPOSITION EXHIBIT B

Website Address: http: www.overlandparkks.org/calendar/YR-1

Kansas City, Kansas Metropolitan Area
Calendar of Events
January 1, YR-1

Health and Fitness: Below is a list of currently scheduled health and fitness events in the area. Check with sponsors for details. (Dates/Times/Locations Subject to Change)

January:	Overland Park Reg. Hosp. Health Expo; January 18; Overland Park Reg. Hosp.
	Exercise Awareness Month Lecture Series; January 24; Civic Center
February:	New Lifestyle Dietetics Exhibition; February 12; Civic Center
March:	Senior Health Expo, March 1; Civic Center
	St. Michael's Hosp. Health Fair; March 10, Convention Center
April:	Kansas City 10K, April 8; Kansas City Plaza
May:	Walk Kansas City, May 6; Kansas City Plaza
	Twin Oaks Hosp. Health Fair; May 10, River Crest Pavilion
June:	Overland Park Reg. Hosp. Health Expo; June 5; Overland Park Reg. Hosp.
July:	July 4 Fun Run; July 4; Kansas City Plaza
	Twin Oaks Hosp. Health Fair; July 8; Valley Crest Park
August:	St. Michael's Hosp. Fitness Screenings; August 14; St. Michael's Hosp.
September:	Twin Oaks Hosp. Health Fair, September 10, Civic Center
	U.S. Military Marathon; September 30; Kansas City Plaza
October:	Greater Kansas City Health Expo; October 14; Civic Center
November:	Twin Oaks Hosp. Health Fair; November 15, River Crest Pavilion
December:	Overland Park Reg. Hosp. Healthy Cooking Lecture Series; December 9; Overland park Reg. Hosp. Cafe

DEPOSITION EXHIBIT C

Website address: http: www.TwinOaksHealthFair.com/YR-1

Free shuttle van service, which can accommodate up to ten passengers, is available for senior citizens to the River Crest Pavilion Complex and the Downtown Civic Center. For pick-up locations and to sign up for the shuttle, click on the link for "Directions and Transportation."

IN THE UNITED STATES DISTRICT COURT
FOR THE DISTRICT OF KANSAS

UNITED STATES OF AMERICA	)	
EX REL.	)	
DAVID E. BARRIER, M.D.,	)	
PLAINTIFF,	)	Civ. Action No. 11-3456-SBM
v.	)	
	)	
TWIN OAKS HOSPITAL, INC.,	)	
DEFENDANT.	)	

DEFENDANT'S MOTION FOR SUMMARY JUDGMENT

Defendant, Twin Oaks Hospital, Inc., by its undersigned counsel, moves this Court, pursuant to Rule 56 of the Federal Rules of Civil Procedure, for an Order granting summary judgment in its favor on Plaintiff's Complaint. Support for this motion is set forth in the accompanying Memorandum of Law, the attached depositions of David E. Barrier, M.D., Julia B. Courtland, Rosemary C. Rinehart, and Andrew M. Crenshaw, M.D., and exhibits thereto.

Respectfully submitted,

Chad Warnock

Chad Warnock
Attorney-in-Charge
Kansas Bar No. 0097643
D. Kan. Bar No. 95462377
Warnock and Bailey
Attorneys at Law
187 Las Cruces Boulevard
Overland Park, Kansas 56788
Telephone: 816-555-6398
Facsimile: 816-555-9852
Email: chadw@wandb.com
Attorney for Defendant
Twin Oaks Hospital, Inc.

Dated: January 11, YEAR

Certificate of Service

I HEREBY CERTIFY that I caused a copy of the foregoing Motion for Summary Judgment and Memorandum of Law in Support of Defendant's Motion for Summary Judgment to be sent via U.S.P.S. Express Mail, postage prepaid, and to be delivered by hand this 11th day of January, YEAR, to counsel for the Plaintiff, Candace Hayes, Esq., Office of Leland, Hayes, and Leland, 4566 Ashleigh Court Plaza, Kansas City, Kansas 64343.

Chad Warnock
Chad Warnock
Attorney-in-Charge
Kansas Bar No. 0097643
D. Kan. Bar No. 95462377
Warnock and Bailey
Attorneys at Law
187 Las Cruces Boulevard
Overland Park, Kansas 56788
Telephone: 316-555-6398
Facsimile: 316-555-9852
Email: chadw@wandb.com
Attorney for Defendant
Twin Oaks Hospital, Inc.

IN THE UNITED STATES DISTRICT COURT
FOR THE DISTRICT OF KANSAS

UNITED STATES OF AMERICA	)	
EX REL.	)	
DAVID E. BARRIER, M.D.,	)	
PLAINTIFF,	)	Civ. Action No. 11-3456-SBM
v.	)	
	)	
TWIN OAKS HOSPITAL, INC.,	)	
DEFENDANT.	)	

**PLAINTIFF'S RESPONSE TO DEFENDANT'S MOTION FOR
SUMMARY JUDGMENT**

Plaintiff/Relator David E. Barrier, M.D., by his undersigned counsel, hereby responds to Defendant's Motion for Summary Judgment, and requests that this Honorable Court deny Defendant's Motion, and in support thereof provides the attached Memorandum of Law in Opposition to Defendant's Motion for Summary Judgment and the attached depositions of David E. Barrier, M.D., Julia B. Courtland, Rosemary C. Rinehart, and Andrew M. Crenshaw, M.D., and exhibits thereto.

Respectfully submitted,

Candace M. Hayes

Candace M. Hayes
Attorney-in-Charge
Kansas Bar No. 910394BJJ
D. Kan. Bar No. 0098765
Office of Leland, Hayes, and Leland
4566 Ashleigh Court Plaza
Kansas City, Kansas 64343
Telephone: 816-900-1029
Facsimile: 816-900-8364
Email:
chayes@lelandhayes.com
Attorney for Plaintiff/Relator
David E. Barrier, M.D.

Dated: January 12, YEAR

Certificate of Service

I HEREBY CERTIFY that I caused a copy of the foregoing Plaintiff's Response to Defendant's Motion for Summary Judgment to be sent via U.S.P.S. Express Mail, postage prepaid, and to be delivered by hand this 12th day of January, YEAR, to counsel for the Defendant, Chad Warnock. Esq., Office of Warnock and Bailey, 187 Las Cruces Boulevard, Overland Park, Kansas 56788.

Candace M. Hayes

Candace M. Hayes
Attorney-in-Charge
Kansas Bar No. 910394BJJ
D. Kan. Bar No. 0098765
Office of Leland, Hayes, and Leland
4566 Ashleigh Court Plaza
Kansas City, Kansas 64343
Telephone: 816-900-1029
Facsimile: 816-900-8364
Email:
chayes@lelandhayes.com
Attorney for Plaintiff/Relator
David E. Barrier, M.D.

ORAL DEFENSE OF AKS MOTION'S BRIEF

Leland, Hayes, and Leland
4566 Ashleigh Court Plaza
Kansas City, Kansas 64343
Telephone: 816-900-1029
Facsimile: 816-900-8364

MEMORANDUM

From: Candace Hayes
To: Associate
Date: Today, YR-1
Re: David E. Barrier, M.D., FCA Claim

Prepare an oral argument of the motion's brief written with regard to the above-referenced matter. The argument will be held in the federal District Court of Kansas. The judge will allot the time limits and the argument protocols set out in the attachment to this letter.

Warnock and Bailey
Attorneys at Law
187 Las Cruces Boulevard
Overland Park, Kansas 56788
Telephone: 316-555-6398
Facsimile: 316-555-9852
Email: chadw@wandb.com

MEMORANDUM

From: Chad Warnock
To: Associate
Date: Today, YR-1
Re: Twin Oaks Hospital matter

Prepare an oral argument of the motion's brief written with regard to the above-referenced matter. The argument will be held in the federal District Court of Kansas. The judge will allot the time limits and the argument protocols set out in the attachment to this letter.

APPELLATE BRIEF: AKS

Leland, Hayes, and Leland
4566 Ashleigh Court Plaza
Kansas City, Kansas 64343
Telephone: 816-900-1029
Facsimile: 816-900-8364

MEMORANDUM

From: Candace Hayes
To: Associate
Date: Today, YR-1
Re: David E. Barrier, M.D., FCA Claim

As you know, Judge Reilly has handed down his order with regard to the above-referenced matter. An appeal has been requested and granted. The order and all appellate documents are attached. Review these materials and draft an appellate brief to the Tenth Circuit.

Warnock and Bailey
Attorneys at Law
187 Las Cruces Boulevard
Overland Park, Kansas 56788
Telephone: 316-555-6398
Facsimile: 316-555-9852
Email: chadw@wandb.com

MEMORANDUM

From: Chad Warnock
To: Associate
Date: Today, YR-1
Re: Twin Oaks Hospital matter

As you know, Judge Reilly has handed down his order with regard to the above-referenced matter. An appeal has been requested and granted. The order and all appellate documents are attached. Review these materials and draft an appellate brief to the Tenth Circuit.

Assignment 17

MEDIATION: AKS

Circuit Mediation Office of
UNITED STATES COURT OF APPEALS FOR
THE TENTH CIRCUIT
The Byron White U.S. Courthouse
1823 Stout Street, Denver, CO 80257
1-303-555-0987

Today, YEAR

Via Electronic and U.S. Mail

Candace Hayes, Esq.
Leland, Hayes, and Leland
4566 Ashleigh Court Plaza
Kansas City, Kansas 64343

Chad Warnock, Esq.
Warnock and Bailey
Attorneys at Law
187 Las Cruces Boulevard
Overland Park, Kansas 56788

Re: <u>Barrier v. Twin Oaks Hospital, Inc.</u>, No. 11-1213

Dear Counsel:

The Circuit Mediation Office of the United States Court of Appeals for the Tenth Circuit has selected this appeal for inclusion in the court's Mediation Program. The mediator assigned to your case is:

Lane Bradley, Esq.
lbb@cmooffice.net

A copy of the mediator's biography is enclosed. If you have any concerns about the impartiality of the assigned mediator, including any bias that might be perceived by others, please email the Circuit Mediation Office at the address listed above immediately. Describe any and all past relationships the assigned mediator has had with counsel, counsel's firm or the parties, and any conflicts you believe the assigned mediator might have.

Assuming no conflict exists, please contact the above-referenced mediator within five days of the date of this letter to discuss the logistics of the conference. To familiarize yourself with the general guidelines of the conference process, you are asked to review the information located at the Mediation Office's website: http://www.ca10.uscourts.gov/cmo/faq.php

The website explains the confidentiality responsibilities of the mediator. All parties, party representatives, attorneys and persons, parties or attorneys assisting them also must maintain confidentiality with respect to any settlement communications made or received during or incident to the mediation process.

Each party is to be represented at the mediation by its principal attorney and by a party representative with actual settlement authority.

Do not hesitate to contact me directly at 303-555-0987 if I may be of further assistance. I wish you success in your conference.

Sincerely,

Celeste Miller
Celeste Miller
Assistant Appellate Conference Attorney

CDM/bdd

cc: Lane Bradley, Esq.

Lane Bradley, Esq.
Circuit Mediation Office
United States Court of Appeals for the Tenth Circuit
The Byron White U.S. Courthouse
1823 Stout Street, Denver, CO 80257
lbb@cmooffice.net

Today, YEAR

<u>*VIA ELECTRONIC AND U.S. MAIL*</u>

Candace Hayes, Esq.
Leland, Hayes, and Leland
4566 Ashleigh Court Plaza
Kansas City, Kansas 64343

Chad Warnock, Esq.
Warnock and Bailey
Attorneys at Law
187 Las Cruces Boulevard
Overland Park, Kansas 56788

Re: <u>Barrier v. Twin Oaks Hospital, Inc.</u>, No. 11-1213

Dear Counsel:

The Circuit Mediation Office of the U.S. Court of Appeals for the Tenth Circuit previously contacted you to let you know that your case is included in the Court's Mediation Program. I will be the mediator for your case, and I look forward to working with you. If at any time during this process you have questions or concerns about the mediation, please let me know and I will be glad to help. Of course, if we fail to settle your case during this scheduled conference, I am available to continue working with you if follow-up discussions or conference sessions seem useful.

This letter serves to confirm the date, time and location for the initial scheduled conference, to give you further details about the conference itself, and to explain what you need to do in preparation.

Date:　　　Month, Day, YEAR, starting at 9:30 A.M.
Location:　TBA

For some of you, this may be the first time you have participated in any settlement conference, while others of you may be familiar with such programs but less familiar with the Tenth Circuit's version of the process. Therefore, please review the information on our website sent to you by the Mediation Office: http://www.ca10.uscourts.gov/cmo/faq.php

The most important aspects of mediation that distinguish it from litigation are the parties' control over the resolution of their dispute and its confidentiality. The conference allows the parties to explore options for resolving their dispute that include but also extend beyond the legal options available in court. Procedurally, the conference program is a flexible process, consisting of a mix of joint sessions and individual caucuses in which parties can discuss the legal and non-legal issues in their dispute, candidly weigh the strengths and weaknesses of their positions, and consider possible legal and non-legal solutions. Throughout this process, confidentiality protects any information related to the case. The fact that a case is in conference is not disclosed to the Court or to the public, and the outcome of the conference is likewise confidential unless all parties agree otherwise. In addition, information that you may disclose during your individual caucuses will not be shared with the other side, except to the extent that you authorize.

Prior to our mediation, I need you to send me the following two documents:

1. A list with the full names of anyone attending the conference on your client's behalf.

2. A Confidential Conference Statement ("CCS") that responds to the issues outlined below. The CCS can be sent by paper to my address above, or via email [lbb@cmooffice.net] or fax (303-555-0988). **Do not send your CCS to the Clerk's Office**. The content of your CCS is confidential and will not be shared with any other party or with the Court.

Other than the conference itself, your preparation of the CCS is the most important element in the conference process. Preparing your CCS allows you, your client, and me, to have a candid view of the factual and legal hurdles that you face, the strengths and weaknesses of both sides' cases, and possible avenues to settlement. Although there is no page limit to a CSS, it is generally 2-4 pages long, depending on the complexity of the issues; it is deliberately intended to be brief but candid and thorough. The Tenth Circuit and its mediators have found that the most useful CCSs follow these guidelines:

A. Please give a brief <u>factual background</u> of the case, indicating any facts that are genuinely in dispute, and why.

B. Identify <u>any cases involving the same parties</u> that are either pending or decided in any tribunal.

C. Identify any controlling or particularly relevant <u>legal authorities</u>. If these authorities are not readily available, please enclose a copy or a link where they can be reviewed.

D. Identify any <u>jurisdictional issues</u> that have been raised by any party, and give your honest assessment of the merits of these claims.

E. Is there any <u>additional information</u> that you need (from the other side, or elsewhere) before agreeing to settle? If so, how might that information be obtained?

F. Give an honest discussion of <u>your claims and defenses</u>. Please identify the strongest and weakest parts of your case and explain—legally or otherwise—their strengths and weaknesses.

G. Give an honest discussion of <u>the strongest and weakest aspects of the other side's case</u>.

H. What, in your candid assessment, is the <u>likely outcome</u> if this case continues to the Fifth Circuit on appeal?

I. Give a brief history of any <u>prior settlement negotiations</u>, and include your candid assessment as to why the case has not settled.

J. Explain any elements that your client <u>cannot compromise</u>. Identify any interests or issues that are not directly involved in this case but that might frustrate or assist in settlement.

K. A list of <u>possible settlement terms and ideas</u>. Alongside each idea, please evaluate candidly the merits of that idea and how it might be achieved.

As you prepare for conference, do not hesitate to contact me if I can be of any assistance. I wish you success in your conference endeavor.

Sincerely,

Lane Bradley
Lane Bradley, Esq.

cc: Celeste Miller

Assignment 18

SETTLEMENT: AKS

Leland, Hayes, and Leland
4566 Ashleigh Court Plaza
Kansas City, Kansas 64343
Telephone: 816-900-1029
Facsimile: 816-900-8364

MEMORANDUM

From: Candace Hayes
To: Associate
Date: Today, YR-1
Re: David E. Barrier, M.D., FCA Claim

As you know, we have reached an agreement with Twin Oaks Hospital, Inc. to settle Dr. Barrier's suit against the hospital. The basic terms of the agreement are reflected in the attachment to this letter.

Please draft a settlement agreement reflecting these terms, and make sure that Dr. Barrier's interests are protected accordingly. Of course, the attorney with the Department of Justice, opposing counsel, and the Court will want to review this document before any of the parties sign.

CH:bb

Warnock and Bailey
Attorneys at Law
187 Las Cruces Boulevard
Overland Park, Kansas 56788
Telephone: 316-555-6398
Facsimile: 316-555-9852
Email: chadw@wandb.com

MEMORANDUM

From: Chad Warnock
To: Associate
Date: Today, YR-1
Re: Twin Oaks Hospital matter

As you know, we have reached an agreement with Dr. David Barrier to settle his suit against the hospital. The basic terms of the agreement are reflected in the attachment to this letter.

Please draft a settlement agreement reflecting these terms, and make sure that Twin Oaks Hospital is protected from any and all future claims with regard to this matter. Pay particular attention to secure compliance with any federal requirements. Of course, opposing counsel and the Court will want to review this document before Dr. Barrier signs.

CW: mc

Assignment 19

TRIAL PRACTICE: AKS

Leland, Hayes, and Leland
4566 Ashleigh Court Plaza
Kansas City, Kansas 64343
Telephone: 816-900-1029
Facsimile: 816-900-8364

MEMORANDUM

From: Candace Hayes
To: Associate
Date: Today, YR-1
Re: Barrier v. Twin Oaks Hospital, Inc.

Prepare for trial in the above-referenced matter, David Barrier's FCA claim. Any of the named witnesses may be called to prove the case. No other witness or information other than that set out below (and exhibits thereto) will be allowed by the court.

1. Deposition of David E. Barrier, M.D.
2. Deposition of Julia Courtland
3. Deposition of Rosemary Rinehart
4. Deposition of Andrew Crenshaw, M.D.

The case is being heard in federal court, in the federal District Court of Kansas. Notification of witnesses and general court rules as to deadlines and other matters, already provided, should be observed at all times.

Warnock and Bailey
Attorneys at Law
187 Las Cruces Boulevard
Overland Park, Kansas 56788
Telephone: 316-555-6398
Facsimile: 316-555-9852
Email: chadw@wandb.com

MEMORANDUM

From: Chad Warnock
To: Associate
Date: Today, YR-1
Re: Barrier v. Twin Oaks Hospital, Inc.

Prepare for trial in the above-referenced matter, Twin Oaks Hospital's defense against David Barrier's FCA action. Any of the named witnesses may be called to rebut Dr. Barrier's claim. No other witness or information other than that set out below (and exhibits thereto) will be allowed by the court.

1. Deposition of David E. Barrier, M.D.
2. Deposition of Julia Courtland
3. Deposition of Rosemary Rinehart
4. Deposition of Andrew Crenshaw, M.D.

The case is being heard in federal court, in the federal District Court of Kansas. Notification of witnesses and general court rules as to deadlines and other matters, already provided, should be observed at all times.